The author at John O'Groats in 2004

LAND'S END TO JOHN O'GROATS

A Thousand Mile Walking Route

Mike Salter

FOLLY PUBLICATIONS

ACKNOWLEDGEMENTS

The following people provided accommodation during our walk in 2004: Eddie Carter & Carol Wiseman in Clevedon, Marjorie & Dennis Salter in Wolverhsmpton, Helen's cousin Diana and her husband Nigel near Leek, Judith and Peter McKinley at Stockport, and Jackie & Mike Jackson at Faugh in Cumbria. Jackie and Mike stored a food parcel for us and have themselves completed the walk (over several years). It was they who suggested using the towpath of the Union Canal and the tracks through the Flow Country from Sutherland into Caithness, lending us maps and notes to help us do this.

Thanks are due to all the people who sponsored Helen Thomas and thus help raise £210 for each of the Woodland Trust, W.W.F, and Worcestershire Wildlife, also to the bed & breakfast proprietors in Dymock and on the Black Isle that dropped their prices when they realised that Helen was doing the walk for charity. We owe a debt of gratitude to half a dozen people who let us camp on their land, particularly the owners of the farm at Bartiestown in an area of NE Cumbria totally devoid of anywhere else to camp or find accommodation. Several other individuals provided us with cups of tea or supplies of drinking water and one family in the Manor Valley provided us with a meal. Thanks also to Paul Adkins for lifts down to Bristol Temple Meads Station.

Helen Thomas took the pictures that appear on pages 7, 15 and 40. All the other pictures are from Mike Salter's own collection of photographs. He also drew the maps.

Although we didn't actually get to meet any of the members of the Backpackers Club until the autumn of 2005, thanks should also go to Christine Roche, the club's magazine editor, and herself author of a book about walking Land's End to John O'Groats, for lots of useful weight-saving ideas discussed in the magazine over the years.

Finally, thanks to the staff at Aspect Design for their help in preparing illustrations and generally assembling the artwork of the book ready for publication.

DISCLAIMER

Every effort has been made to ensure information in this book is accurate and up-to-date, but the author/publisher does not accept any responsibility for any accidents to users, nor is any responsibility accepted for any problems that might arise through any of the information given being inaccurate, incomplete or out-of-date. Please take careful note of the suggestions about outdoor safety given on page 14.

Note that whilst blockages on roads will normally be cleared within a day or two any obstructions on paths do not get this sort of priority. There is a good chance you will have to make a diversion at some point because of an obstruction, flooding, or the collapse of paths, trees or bridges. An example of this is the very long line of fallen conifers currently blocking (with no possible easy diversion) a good and newly-signed forest path at NH 482592 (just north of Strathpeffer) which would otherwise provide a possible connection between the main route at Contin and the eastern alternative route at Evanton.

AUTHOR"S NOTES

Distances are given in miles, still the most familiar unit of measurement for most British people. Although modern Ordnance Survey maps are metric, heights and amounts of climb in this book are given in feet, mainly so as to avoid any ambiguity as to whether an m folowing a figure means miles or metres. The contours on the Landranger maps are at 10 metre intervals, ie crossing three of them means roughly 100 feet of climb.

ABOUT THE AUTHOR

Mike Salter is 53 and has been a professional author and publisher since 1988. He is particularly interested in the planning and layout of medieval; buildings and has a huge collection of plans of castles and old churches he has measured during tours (mostly by bicycle and motorcycle) throughout all parts of the British Isles since 1968. Woilver-hampton born and bred, Mike now lives in an old cottage beside the Malvern Hills. Since walking Land's End to John O'Groats in 2004 following his 50th birthday he has done many other long distance backpacking trails. He is a life member of both the YHA and English Heritage, and he is also a member of the Backpackers Club and the Mountain Bothies Association. His other interests include railways, board games, morris dancing and calling folk dances and playing percussion with an occasional ceilidh band.

Chepstow Castle

CONTENTS

INTRODUCTION

There is no single definitive route from Land's End to John O'Groats, either for motorists, cyclists, or wslkers. The log-books kept in the hotels at either end show that most of those who make the journey and manage to log it actually travel by bicycle using the roads. In each year only forty or fifty people will complete the end-to-end journey on foot. Those intent upon walking it in the fastest possible time (journeys of 12 to 13 days have been recorded), or achieving stunts such as pushing wheelbarrows will only use the roads. The famous "naked rambler", delayed by being constantly arrested, arrived in Caithness in January 2004, and a few months before him someone managed it carrying a door the whole way. The signposts at either end give the minumum road distance as 874 miles, although the building of the Forth Road Bridge has taken six miles off that.

Popular interest in walking from Land's End to John O'Groats really took off following Dr Barbara Moore's completion of the journey in 22 days in 1960, which inspired holiday camp owner Billy Butlin to put on a race with £5000 prize money. Of 715 entrants that set off from John O'Groats in late February 1961 only 138 made it to Land's End.

This book, however, assumes that you are not treating the journey as a race and that you want a route that uses mostly traffic-free paths and tracks, which traverse wonderful scenery with places and features of interest to stop and look at, and yet a route which is relatively easy to follow, without a lot of mud, bog, unfordable streams, or having to scramble over rocks, walls, or fences. Also there should at reasonable intervals be places where supplies and services can be found, and accommodation for non-campers. The author considers the route described to offer the best compromise between these sometimes conflicting considerations. The scenery on the route described will mostly vary between pleasant and superb, yet the amount of up and down is kept to a minimum, generally without frequent steep climbs and descents except on just a few days.

Although it is hoped that readers will be able to use long sections of the route as described, there is no expectation that anyone will exactly follow every mile of the described route from start to finish. There will always be a few days when, either out of necessity or whimsy, going a different way to that described here will seem to make sense. In any case a number of alternatives are discussed, partly because the main route described has two long sections in the Scottish Highlands without any facilities which only those carrying camping equipment and several days food will be able to follow.

Accompanied by Helen Thomas, the author walked from Land's End to John O'Groats in the spring of 2004, taking 72 days (including five days of little or no walking) to cover 972 miles, giving an average of 14 miles per day of actual walking. Only about a third of the route then used coincides with the route described here, since the 2004 route contained over 400 miles of road-walking, and diversions to visit friends and relatives. Since completion of the walk on 12th June 2004 the author has since been working on finding alternative traffic-free trails with the aim of publishing a route of about a thousand miles with not much more than 200 miles on tarmac. Some road walking is unavoidable, especially in and out of towns and villages, and there's not much in the way of paths in Caithness that aren't dead ends. Access to shops, stations, b&bs, hostels, campsites, etc, nearly always involves some walking along busy roads, or at least on pavements or verges beside such roads. Mike and Helen walked the West Highland Way in May 2005, and the section from Bristol to the Malvern Hills in April 2006, whilst Mike walked the other new sections alone at various times during 2006.

Men An Tol, Cornwall   *Blaise Castle Folly, near Bristol*

The Falkirk Wheel in operation moving narrow boats from one level to another

The route described takes in a large number of old churches and other ancient monuments. Over a hundred of these heritage sites lie on or very close to the route. Nothing more than about a mile and a half from the route is mentioned unless its particularly important, on a possible diversionary route that doesn't significantly increase the amount of overall mileage, or which is likely to be visited by those having to make minor diversions anyway to find accommodation, eg those seeking hostels in Bristol. Descriptions of heritage sites are mostly kept brief as it was considered important to keep this book as small and light as possible. Readers wanting more detail about castles and churches should consult the more detailed books covering most of the route already published by Mike Salter. See details inside the back cover. The churches make useful check points to and from which mileages are given, and they can sometimes be used as navigational aids when crossing fields on poorly deliniated paths. In most cases you can shelter in their porches to eat your lunch or sort out your pack. The circles with dots in them on the maps show churches, not the village centres, which may be up to a mile away.

The amount of detail about the actual walking route varies somewhat throughout the book. The coast-path of Devon and Cornwall is very clearly signposted and has been described in detail in other publications so only the inland sections cutting off headlands require much detailed description. To some degree the same is true of the West Highland Way and the short lengths of the Pennine Way which are used, plus also the several sections of canal towpath, where navigation is particuarly easy. More detail was needed for the Macmillan, Gloucestershire and Staffordshire ways. They are well signed in some parts. However, where the Gloucestershire Way joins a road there is never any indication of which way to go along the road, and also there's one or two short bits of heathland with a confusing array of criss-cross paths.

Starting the walk at Land's End and finishing at John O'Groats has two distinct advantages. Firstly, for much of the walk the sun and the prevailing south-westerly wind will be behind you. Secondly, if you start in Cornwall in March or April the spring will effectively move northwards with you so that the extremes of winter and summer weather may be avoided. Spring is a good time to see fauna and flora. Also, in the Scottish Highlands there's only a few weeks between when the weather improves and the days lengthen in April and May, and when midges become a problem in early June, especially for camping in sheltered low-level spots beside water. Departing Land's End in March in the hope of arriving in Caithness by the end of May is recommended. Note that in Scotland in May there will probably still be patches of snow over the 2500ft level, especially on north facing slopes, and frosts and snow showers are still a distinct possibility.

DISCUSSION OF POSSIBLE ALTERNATIVE ROUTES

England now has a large number of long-distance paths and by stringing a series of them together you can create a route from Land's End up to Scotland that involves only short and infrequent sections of road-walking. Recognised long-distance paths have the advantage of sometimes being better signed and maintained than other paths, but they are designed simply as attractive routes for recreation rather than the shortest distance between two points, so they are not necessarily the most efficient way of travelling the length of the country within a few weeks.

Its possible to string together the north coast paths of Cornwall, Devon, and Somerset, then use the Macmillan Way over the Quantocks towards Glastonbury and Bath to pick up the Cotswold Way from there to Chipping Campden. You can then use the Cotswold Way, the Heart of England Way and the Limestone Way to reach the start of the Pennine Way at Edale. An alternative is to walk most or all of the Offa's Dyke Path from Chepstow and then cut across Cheshire to the Penine Way. In Scotland the St Cuthbert's Way links the end of the Pennine Way at Kirk Yetholm with the Southern Upland Way at Melrose, although Dere St can be used to cut off a corner. There's no offical link between the Southern Upland Way and any route leading north and there's no official traffic-free route north of Inverness, but the towpaths of the Union and Clyde and Forth Canals provide access from Edinburgh to within a few miles of the start of the West Highland Way from Milmgavie to the foot of Ben Nevis, and from there the Great Glen Way provides access up to Inverness.

The route described above adds up to well over 1200 miles. The idea behind the trail described in this book is to use just parts of several of these long-distance ways to produce a shorter route which is just as scenic, with added attractions of its own, but without all the very steep ups and downs of doing all of the coast paths, Offa's Dyke and Pennine Way It reduces the amount of winding around rather than heading northwards which is a feature of parts of the Cotswold and Pennine Ways, avoiding bleak and boggy sections on the Pennine Way, and minimising mileage cutting across fields of arable crops or long, wet grass, although some of this is, of course, unavoidable.

A more central route across Cornwall, Devon and Somerset takes in the delights of Bodmin Moor and the northern edge of Dartmoor and there are lovely old churches at fairly short intervals, but this route means up to 60% road walking since many of the inland paths are little used, overgrown and hard to follow. Following inland paths or lanes will involve intense map-reading for almost every mile. The north coast route almost entirely on paths is well signed and easy to follow but involves a lot of steep 400 - 500ft climbs and descents back down to sea-level, particularly between Bude and Clovelly. The route described compromises between these two alternatives, using much of the coast paths but cutting off several headlands, and then, after the Quantock Hills and Bridgwater there's a change of scene crossing the Somerset Levels.

The suspension bridsge over the Clifton Gorge is well worth seeing, the access to it in and out of Bristol suburbia being surprisingly pleasant. The Severn Way and the Gloucester and Sharpness canal can provide flat, easy walking east of the River Severn all the way from Aust up to Bewdley via Gloucester, Tewkesbury and Worcester, but the trail described in this book uses several other flat sections on canal towpaths both in England and Scotland, so a more exciting route is followed here. This involves crossing the Severn Bridge to Chepstow, which has one of the most spectacular of Welsh castles, walking a short section of Offa's Dyke, then across the Forest of Dean via an interesting sculpture trail, over May Hill, and along the beautiful Malvern Hills and the wonderful ridgeway walking of the Worcestershire Way all the way to Bewdley.

A route alternating between mostly well-maintained sections of canal towpath, good paths and tracks over the heathlands of Kinver Edge and Cannock Chase, and an old railway line past Rudyard Lake offers good and most easy walking up as far as Delph. Its easier than the Heart of England Way, which crosses lots of fields, and bypasses the difficult first part of the Pennine Way over Kinder Scout. The Pennine Way is joined later but instead of going east to Middleton-in-Teesdale an easy to follow cut-off ipassing several interesting castles is provided via Kirkby Stephen and Appleby. The Pennine Way is then rejoined for a climb over Cross Fell, the highest point of the main route and the only mountain summit over 2000ft which is traversed.

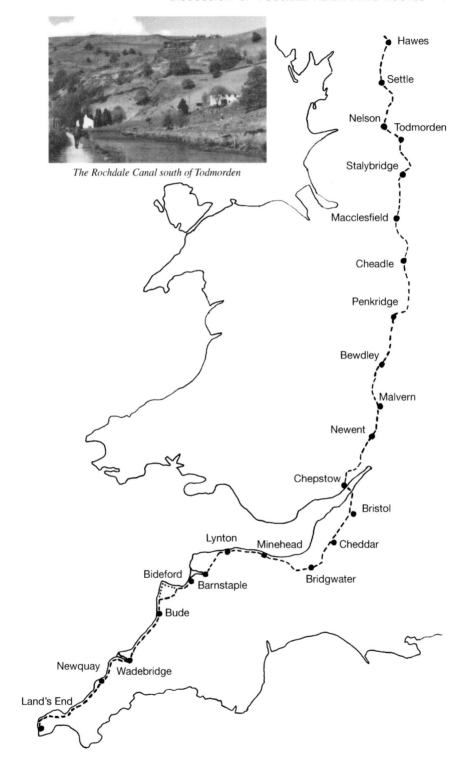

The Rochdale Canal south of Todmorden

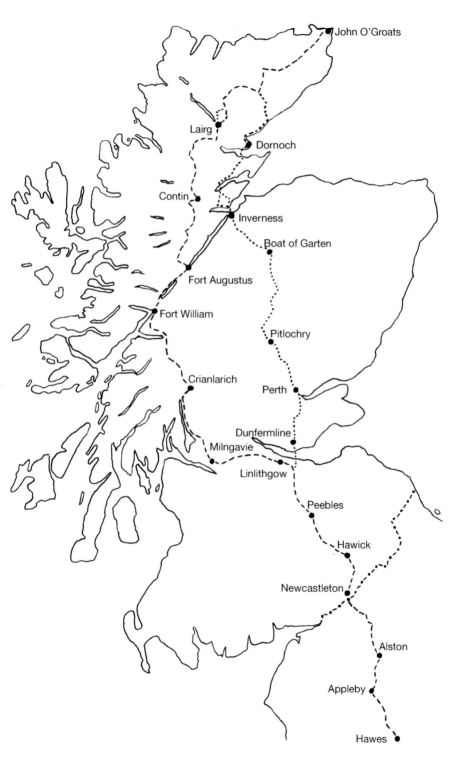

The route described here between Hadrian's Wall and Peebles is a fairly direct and lovely walk through some wild country with several interesting castles and other monuments, but it will require greater navigional skill than any of the sections of the route further south. What are the alternatives? The bleak and boggy Cheviots section of the Pennine Way is the only way of crossing into Scotland without any road-walking, but its end at Kirk Yetholm lies considerably to the east of any of the possible routes leading to the north end of Scotland. Scotland bends such that Edinburgh on its east coast actually lies slightly further west than Carlisle on the English west coast. Going through the middle of the Lake District and up to Carlisle might seem tempting, but you are then faced with a dreary 40-mile road walk from Carlisle to Beattock. The straight, wide and fairly flat side-roads of south Dumfriesshire pass hardly any places to stay or camp, and are a far cry from the hilly, winding, narrow leafy lanes of Devon and Cornwall, where traffic cannot safely attain much speed. There's a similar situation in Lanarkshire, so heading up directly through from Beattock into the Clyde Valley and onto Glasgow isn't attractive either, although the Clyde Walkway provides a mostly traffic-free route to Milngavie from Bothwell Castle. Crossing the Border at Canonbie and heading up to Peebles via Langholm and Ettrick also involves a lot of road walking, although that route is fairly scenic.

From the Union Canal towpath near Niddry Castle two alternative routes up to Kinbrace in Sutherland are given in this book. One uses canal towpaths to reach Milngavie, then the clearly signed West Highland Way and Great Glen Way to Fort Augustus, after which there's tracks via Cannich, Contin, Garve and Lairg to reach Kinbrace. This 300 mile section only uses about 40m of roads but beyond Contin there's two sections up to 36m long without any means of access (even via trains or buses) to accommodation. The other route crosses the Forth Bridge and goes up through Perth, Dunkeld, Pitlochry, Blair Atholl, Inverness, Alness, Tain, Dornoch and Golspie to Kinbrace. This route is 65 miles shorter, but well over a hundred miles of it is on roads and tarmac cycle-tracks beside (or close to) the noisy A9. The Dunkeld to Blair Atholl section is quite pretty though. On this route non-campers will have to do extra miles to divert eastwards either to Inverey youth hostel or B&Bs in Braemar, and on the following day will either have to return to the A9 at Aviemore or do a 26m day from Inverey over Lairig Ghru to Boat of Garten.

Quite a lot of people reach Pitlochry and then Glen Tilt via Aberfeldy despite the fact that only parts of the Wade military north road from Crieff are walkable, involving a five mile section and two shorter sections of walking along A826 from Amulree. The author crossed the Forth on Kincardine Bridge, taking delightful paths past Castle Campbell and Glendevon Youth Hostel to Auchterader, but then having to use dull roads to Fowlis Wester, from which there's tracks to reach the Wade road up to Amulree. Others have used a few miles of the Fife Coastal Path, then north either via Kinross or the Lomond Hills, and then NW from Bridge of Earn to Muthil to avoid the suburbia of Perth.

Since the coastal route north of Inverness is nearly all road walking, using a route from the Forth Bridge to John O'Groats via Dalwhinnie, Inverness and Tain means you'll hardly ever escape from the noise of traffic anywhere north of the Pentland Hills. There's a possible 20 mile inland route from Alness to Ardgay via Ardross Castle, but the path towards Dornoch Firth from Strath Rusdale is boggy and hard to follow. A lack of services on remote inland routes in Ross and Sutherland means that those unwilling to carry camping gear and several days' food will have to keep close to the coast beyond Inverness. Crossing from Sutherland into Caithness they will be forced to walk several miles actually on the A9 itself, two sections being without even verges or pavements. It is, of course, possible to combine parts of the two described routes, continuing further northeast up the Great Glen from Fort Augustus, either to Inverness, or cutting across from Drumnadrochit to Beauly and Muir or Ord to reach Alness.

From Kinbrace one alternative is to follow A897 up to the north coast and then walk on or beside A 836 to Thurso. This makes shopping easier (although reaching the shop near Melvich involves rather a detour), and it allows a visit to Dunnet Head, the most northerly point on the mainland, near which short sections of shore path can be used.

Do not try heading to Fort Augustus from Blair Atholl. It involves 30 miles of walking on or beside A9 and A889 to Laggan for the start of the Wade Road over Corrieyairack Pass. The Dalwhinnie to Feagour route is very difficult (boggy moor and dense forest).

PLANNING YOUR WALK

1. HOW LONG WILL IT TAKE?

Most people think in tems of a thousand mile walk taking between ten and thirteen weeks. Few people will be able to walk such a distance in less than eight weeks. Some time will probaby be spent on visiting places of interest, shopping, washing clothes, and socialising with friends and relatives you stay with. Medical problems or repair or replacement of important items of equipment are likely to cause delays or diversions.

Because of the difficulties involved in leaving jobs and homes for long periods some people do walks of this sort in stages, sometimes spreading the journey over more than one year. Bear in mind that this will greatly increase your transport costs, although this may not be a problem if the stages really are spread over several years.

2. HOW DIFFICULT IS IT?

Obviously you need to be fit, and used to carrying a rucksack. The author was 50 when he did the walk and hadn't done much backpacking for twenty years, although he had kept fit through doing cycling, dancing and shorter walks. His companion had virtually no previous experience of backpacking and had generally done only short walks exercising her dogs around her village. Your mental attitude is as important as level of fitness since you'll need to cope with aches and pains, poor weather, periods of insufficient sleep, and times when accommodation or resupply points haven't worked out as hoped for.

The walk described attempts to minimise the amount of steep climbing that has to be done in so far as it's possible to do this without a lot of extra road-walking or missing out on fine scenery or places that are worth visiting. The first two weeks will be the toughest, partly because your body will still be getting used to this level of exercise, and partly because the coastal paths of Cornwall and Devon have more steep climbs than will be experienced elsewhere along the walk. Elsewhere where possible the walk either uses low level routes, or climbs up onto ridgeway paths heading north for many miles.

3. RIGHTS OF WAY AND NAVIGATION

Up as far as Hadrian's Wall the route described generally uses paths and tracks that are marked on Ordnance Survey maps as being Public Rights of Way. A few short sections across arable fields may not be marked on the ground, but usually a distant stile or post, or a landmark such as a church tower, indicates where to head for. Between Birdoswald on Hadrian's Wall and Peebles there are four high moorland sections each up to two and a half miles long where greater navigational skills are required. There are also a couple of longer moorland sections much further north which require some navigational skills.

Scottish law allows walkers greater access. Prohibitive signs on estate roads and on tracks in forests where tree-felling is taking place refer to vehicles. Wslkers can usually go anywhere, provided you do not meddle with anything, or cause any obstruction, and that you obey the country code..The route described in Scotland mostly has gates that will open and generally uses paths and tracks that are clearly defined on the ground. Paths in Scotland go round arable fields rather than diagonally cut across them as in England. Expect the occasional locked gate and low fence in the way, but on the whole there will less obstructions in Scotland than on English paths with their frequent high and narrow stiles and old kissing gates that sometimes don't allow room for your backpack.

4. AVAILABILITY OF FOOD AND DRINK

In England there will never be more than about 20 miles between places with shops so you don't need to carry more than two days' dood. In the Borders there's a 30m gap between Hawick and Peebles, On the main route there's gaps of 32m between Fort William and Fort Augustus, 28m Cannich to Contin, 53m between Contin and Lairg, and then no proper shop for 95m to John O'Groats. On the eastern route there's a 41m gap between Blair Atholl and Boat of Garten, and an 82m gap between Golspie and John O'Groats. One hotel and access to railway stations do ease the situation on this last section.

Public toilets are frequent on the coast paths of Cornwall, Devon and Somerset, but most of them now have wall units rather than sinks with taps. Further north you'll mostly only see one set of public toilets each day. On some days obtaining drinking water may be difficult and you may occasionally need to carry a couple of litres a few miles if you are wild camping. Give considerable thought as to how you can do this comfortably.

5. HOSTELS AND B&B ACCOMMODATION

At the time of writing several small youth hostels along the route are under threat of closure. Despite this it should be possible to find accommodation at intervals mainly of 12 to 18 miles in England, although a 20 mile day may be needed to cross the Severn Bridge, and some B&Bs may lie two or three miles off the direct route. In Scotland you will occasionally need to walk a 20 or 22 mile day, and the east route via Blair Atholl and Lairig Ghru means a diversion and a pair of 24 and 26 mile days. North of the Great Glen only the coastal route offers accommodation at close enough intervals for non-campers. This means many miles on busy roads, and in Sutherland and Caithness you'll need to do one or two shuttles back and forwards on the trains to obtain any accommodation.

6. CAMPING PLACES

Camp-sites are plentiful in Cornwall, Devon and Somerset, there's one in the middle of Bristol, and another beside the route near Newent. Further north there's a site at Gailey (north of Wolverhampton), and others near Macclesfield, Earby, Settle, Hawes and Kirkby Stephen. In Scotland there are camp-sites close to the Union and Forth & Clyde canals, several beside the West Highland Way, and others at Fort Augustus, Contin, Lairg and John O'Groats. In between these either use other forms accommodation or wild camp. Joining the Backpackers Club, the Caravan & Camping Club and the Mountain Bothies Association will give you information on camp-sites and bothies not otherwise advertised. Any huts mentioned in the Scottish sections of route should be open but some may be quite rough inside so not all of them are suitable for sleeping in.

Camping out in wild places without any facilities is great fun, saves money and will save having to make diversions off the route. Always obtain prior verbal permission from landowners for camping if possible. In England you may well need to call in at the nearest farm anyway to obtain drinking water. Do not drink water that's run over arable land possibly treated with chemicals, or which may have been polluted by cattle or drainage from buildings. In West Yorkshire, Cumbria and the Scottish mountains you should be able to find remote places to camp where there's water safe to drink close at hand.

In England there are many places where wild camping contravenes bylaws, such as on National Trust land and the Malvern Hills. Its unlikely you'll be arrested for camping, unless you are causing damage or some other serious nuisance, but you could be moved on. It is legal to stop for rest or refreshment whilst walking along a right-of-way but there is no right to erect any sort of shelter, however temporary. The basic rule about wild camping is to be discreet. Use a tent with a flysheet of a colour that blends with its surroundings, and (except in remote or secluded places) pitch fairly late, eave early, and don't light fires. Don't leave rubbish, make noise, or pitch close to, or within sight of, roads or houses, or in fields with animals, especially cows. Finding places to wild camp isn't always easy as much terrain is too steep, too rough or rocky, overgrown or overlooked. Also finding shelter from the wind and any drinkable water can be a problem.

7. OTHER SERVICES

In England towns at Newquay, Bideford, Barnstaple, Bridgwater, Minehead, Macclesfield, Settle, and Appleby, plus Chepstow in Wales, all on or within a mile of the main route, offer all services i.e. supermarkets, health food shops, bakeries, markets, post ofices, pharmacies, outdoor equipment shops, banks and cash-points, restaurants, take-away food places, B&Bs, tourist informatiion offices, railway stations (or hourly rail-connected buses), police stations, doctors and dentists). The same services are available within three miles of the route at Bristol, Malvern and Wolverhampton. Lynton, Cheddar, Bewdley, Cheadle, Stalybridge, Hyde, Nelson and Hawes also offer a fair range of services.

In the Scottish Borders there's just Hawick and Peebles offering all services (except trains). On the western route only Falkirk and Fort William offer all services further north, with a lesser range of services at Milngavie and Kinlochleven. On the east route all services are provided at Dunfermline, Perth, Pitlochry and Inverness, with a lesser range of services at Kinross, Dunkeld, Alness, Tain and Golspie. Trains can be taken from and to at least a dozen places on this route north of the Forth Road Bridge. Elsewhere services such as shops, hostels and camp-sites are mentioned where they are available. Note that hardware stores will usually sell meths, gas, and possibly tent pegs (or skewers).

EQUIPMENT

1. MAPS

Depending on what route you eventually follow, you could need up to 38 of the Ordnance Survey 1:50.000 Landranger maps. Together all these maps will weigh 4kg and take up more space in your pack than a sleeping bag. However there's several maps where only a corner or edge is needed so consider options such as photocopying (but note copyright restrictions) or just printing out the bits of map you need from a computer programme. Post maps ahead of you if possible, and certainly post home used maps after you've used a highlighter on them to record your route. Linear maps and guide books containing maps available for the Devon & Cornwall coast paths and the West Highland Way, etc, may be a way of saving weight on maps for these sections.

You could buy maps as you travel, but this will need a lot of cash, doesn't allow easy pre-planning to check where B&Bs, hostels and campsites are before you start out, and there's a risk of being held up or getting lost because you couldn't obtain the next map. Generally, you shouldn't need any 1:25,000 maps. Hopefully the information in this book will help in the handful of places where the route is tricky to follow on a 1:50,000 scale map. Its a good idea to have a waterproof case to carry a map or two, plus this book and any other notes so you can check things even in wet and windy conditions.

2. NAVIGATIONAL AIDS

A particularly useful item is a Global Positioning System. You can check your speed and distance, and time travelled, but best of all it will give you a grid reference accurate to a few feet. This is very useful on heathlands criss-crossed with lots of paths to enable you to check where to turn off, etc. Its easy enough to make navigational errors on lowland paths through farmland in Staffordshire in good weather let alone in bad weather on high exposed boggy moors or in the extensive forests found further north. Those who like treasure hunting can additionally use the unit to find geocaches (website details given on page 76), of which there are many along the route. GPS units tend to use up batteries quickly, and don't work too well in dense forests since they need a clear view of the sky, so you'll need a compass and good map-reading skills as well.

3. FOOTWEAR

A thousand mile walk is longer than the life-expectantcy of most boots, especially the cheaper ones, so its a good idea to have a second pair already purchased and worn in if you are planning to break the journey with a day or two at home. A remote section of the Highlands is not the place to discover a split in your boots! It may be worth carrying a pair of proper trekking sandals, although they will weigh about 600g. These are useful for several possible walks across beaches, for fording any burns in Scotland that are swollen by heavy rain, and in hot weather they may also be used for some lengthy sections on roads and along old railway lines, etc, where the surfaces are good and ankle-support is less important. They will also be useful for indoors if you are planning to stay in lots of hostels, pubs, private houses, etc, Your boots will probably weigh 600g more than your sandals so try not to carry them in or on your pack for long distances, especially if you are carrying several days food. Carry enough socks to last three days, just in case wet weather delays drying times.

4. TREKKING POLES

Use of a pair of trekking poles is recommended. They enable the arms to do much of the work of propelling you forwards, especially on steep climbs. Having two means that you can use them as crutches if you hurt a leg or an ankle in a remote place and can't summon any assistance. Campers can save weight by carrying a tent or tarp which uses trekking poles for uprights such as the Mountain Equipment Ultralite. Trekking poles are also useful for getting over stiles, fording streams, pushing brambles and nettles out of the way and for defence against hostile animals.

5. MEDICAL KIT

This should contain both ordinary plasters and ones designed specifically for blisters on your feet. You should also have a bandage, safety pins, antiseptic cream, general-purpose painkillers, cloves or Bonjela (for toothache), and medication for diarrhoea such as Imodium. You are also likely to need an ointment for muscular aches such as Ibuleve or Deep Heat. Vaseline is useful to rub onto sore feet,.

OTHER GENERAL ITEMS OF EQUIPMENT

Emergency Blanket: Silver foil cover to keep you warm in case of fall in remote place.
Gaiters: Keeps your legs and feet dry when walkiing through long grass or mud.
Insect Repellant: Essential after the midge season starts in early June in Scotland.
Mirror: You may be able to save weight by carrying a combined mirror and hair-brush.
Mobile Phone: Essential for emergencies and making accommodation bookings, etc.
You may not be able to get a signal in some places in the Scottish Highlands.
Rucksack Cover: Use either a rucksack inner liner or outer cover, or both.
Sewing Kit: Suitable threads for repairs to clothing, rucksack, tent, etc.
A small roll of cloth-backed tape is also useful for all kinds of repair jobs..
Toilet Paper: You should also carry a light trowel for burying used paper & excrement.
Toiletries: Carry small quantities of soaps & shampoos in old film containers, etc.
Towel: Use a special lightweight camping towel for minimal space and weight.
Umbrella: Of little use on exposed ridges, but useful on sheltered woodland paths.
Utensils: You'll need these sooner or later even if not camping.
Water Bottles: Try using a pair of one litre Platypus bottles, which go flat when empty.
Whistle: Traditional means of summoning help in case of an accident.
Writing Equipment: Pens, highlighter to mark map, ruler to measure mileages on map.
You may also want to carry a camera, binoculars, hat, gloves, swimming costume, torch, scissors. Campers will also need: Sleeping Bag, Inflatable Mat, Stove, Cooking Pans, Cup, Matches, Clothes Pegs, Pan Scrubber.

WEIGHT SAVING HINTS, PARTICULARLY FOR CAMPERS

Weigh everything that goes in your pack. Leave behind all non-essentials and find lighter alternatives wherever possible. It really is worth it, you may be carrying this pack for over twelve weeks! You can't afford to carry lots of clothing. Carry little, and wash it often, so make sure its light and quick drying. Use clothes with a proper wicking system, rather than your favourite old T-shirts and sweatshirts. The extra expense is worth it.

Wearing waterproof clothing (eg the Paramo ranges) saves having to carry extra spare clothes and waterproofs in your pack. It also saves opening the pack to find waterproofs when it starts to rain. This sort of clothing may be too warm in high summer, although the trousers have side vents and jackets can be worn tied around the waist instead of in your pack. Most of the time only a single baselayer is needed under the jackets when you are walking with a pack on, but carry extra layers as needed.

Try not to carry tins, The contents will often weigh 450g,the empty tin alone 70g, and you may have to carry the empty tin a long way until you see a rubbish bin. Consider buying a dehydrator. Dried foods will last several weeks, weigh very little, and can be carried in small plastic bags weighing nothing. You could post parcels of dried food ahead to post offices, hostels or friends you are planning to stay with. Buying packets of ready dried meals from outdoor shops is very expensive and not recommended

Try carrying items that are heavy, valuable or likely to be needed quickly (such as drinks, snacks, camera and binoculars) on a waist-belt or in a bum-bag across your chest rather than in your main pack. Check carefully that this is robust & comfortable.

Meths is cheaper, easier to obtain, and lighter than gas canisters (the canisters alone weigh 65g. Remember though that meths stoves are a bit slower and not so safe to use within the confines of a porch of a tent. Never cook inside the main tent itself.

Post home all surplus maps and guides, souvenirs purchased en route, and any items of equipment that prove to be superfluous. The weight saving really is worth the cost and trouble and the items are more likely to get damaged in your pack than in the post.

Try to keep your total pack weight under 9kg (roughly 20lbs) not including food, water and fuel. Its possible to get this weight down to 5 or 6kg for weekend trips, but when walking for more than a few days you will probably need more clothes and socks, a deodorant, swimming costume, sandals, more maps and guides, shaving gear, and other extra items which will increase the weight of your pack. Food for a whole day will normally weigh almost 1kg, especially if you carry bread, but using Ryvitas, oatcakes and dried foods may reduce this to about 750g per day. Even when using dried foods enough supplies to give a safety margin in case of delay for a seven day trek away from all shops will weigh over 5kg, so your pack could then weigh at least 14kg (37lbs) in total.

OUTDOOR SAFETY

Make sure you are wearing footwear suitable for the nature of the terrain and that you have enough dry clothes to remain warm enough even in the most stormy conditions. Always carry an emergency blanket to keep the body warm enough in case of an accident. Stop and sort out any problems with your feet or boots immediately. Take care on cliff-top paths with sheer drops and consider using nearby lanes instead if the conditions are very windy. Carrying a tiny radio and listening to weather forcasts may help you to make safer decisions as to which route to use or what type of accomodation to try for. When walking on roads face the oncoming traffic, ie the righthand side of the road.

Even on well signed paths it's important to keep note of where you are on the map. If you need help you may need to be able to give a grid reference quickly in order for emergency services to arrive promptly. If you have to leave someone in order to get help try to make sure they have enough food and drink for several hours and that they will be warm enough. Carry enough food and drink so that you don't have to rush unduly or take risks or dodgy shortcuts. Running down slopes can cause erosion and is more likely to lead to accidents. There is a risk of being stranded and possibly even drowning if you mis-time a short-cut taken across a beach. If in doubt stay above high tide level. Don't drink water or eat any foodstuffs gathered or found by the wayside unless you are sure it is safe to do so.

Be realistic when estimating times and distances. Very few people can walk at more than three miles an hour for any period of time even on a straight and level road or track. On rocky, meandering river-side paths cross-crossed by tree-roots or on steep uphill sections of path distances will be further than they appear to be on an Ordnance Survey map and you are not likely to do much more than two miles an hour, including short stops. Even for strong walkers on comparatively easy terrain twenty miles will usually take eight hours to cover, including short stops, twenty-five miles will take ten or eleven hours, and thirty miles is unlikely to be covered in less than thirteen hours. A two and a half mile section on boggy moorland where there's little obvious path, necessitating frequent stops to check the map or GPS could take two hours in bad weather conditions and add an extra hour to your estimated time of arrival. By late May and early June it will light until about 22.00hrs in Scotland and there's eighteen hours of daylight, but if you start in Cornwall in March before British Summer Time begins it will be dark before 19.00hrs, and there's only twelve hours of daylight available. Remember to allow some time for jobs such as washing and wringing out clothing, shopping and maintaining equipment.

ENVIRONMENTAL IMPACT

Basically: Leave nothing but footprints, take nothing but photographs & memories. So:
Don't leave any litter, even biodegradable material such as fruit cores and skins.
Don't pick flowers or damage trees & plants, except where necessary to clear a path.
Don't make lots unecessary noise, especially when passing through farmyards.
Don't get so close to animals that they become stressed and abandon their young.
Don't stray from the right of way, assuming, of course, you can clearly see its route.
Don't touch farming or forestry equipment, crops, timber stacks or building materials.
Leave all gates as you find them, whether open or closed..
Be discreet if wild camping (see page 11), and guard against all risk of accidental fires.

Use public toilets where possible. If you have to go outdoors make sure you are at least 30m from running water and bury excrement in a small hole where it will decompose quicker. Do not bury tampons or sanitary towels. You will have to carry these out. Ideally you should also do this with toilet paper also, since it doesn't decompose quickly and will blow around if dug up by animals.

Try to support local businesses where possible. This puts money into the pockets of local people who keep the countryside running, rather than making profits for huge urban-based corporations.

Taking a dog on a trip such as this will be difficult as it will not be welcome in hostels or some of the B&Bs or campsites. There are some short sections of the route where there are restrictions on dogs. In any case, if you do take a dog with you it should be under very close control at all times so as not to disturb other animals and other walkers.

GETTING TO LAND'S END TO MAKE A START

There's an hourly bus service to Land's End from the bus station at Penzance, which lies beside the railway station there, and the bus ride will usually take about 50 minutes. The road leading from the bus and rail stations up into the town of Penzance passes by most of the type of shops you'll need if you've forgotten anything. Getting to Penzance by train takes five hours from London, four hours from Bristol, six hours from Birmingham, and eleven hours from Edinburgh even on the quickest possible timings. The National Express coaches are cheaper, but take even longer, although unlike the trains they do travel right throughout the night. In short, most or all of a day will be taken up in reaching Land's End, since even someone leaving Bristol around 9am will not get to Land's End much before 3pm, even if they manage to get a bus almost immediately after leaving the railway station. Many people stay overnight nearby so the first walking day is a full one.

Land's End is very touristy now, with lots of souvenirs on sale, and there's toilets, a cafe, food kiosks, and a hotel, where there's a register of End-to-Enders that you should sign if you have time. There's a similar register in the hotel at John O'Groats. The nearest food-shops to Land's End are a mile away at Sennen, south of which is the nearest camp-site. The youth hostel named as Land's End and the Kelynack bunkbarn lie four or five miles northwards from Land's End, so if you are not camping you need to work out if you can arrive at Land's End early enough to walk the first few miles to either of these hostels before dark. This is particularly important if you are starting out in March before the clocks go forward to British summer-time and it may be dark by about 6pm. Other options are to the stay the night in either Penzance or St Ives, which both have plenty of B&Bs, hotels and independant hostels, and then go out to Land's End in the morning.

The Nine Maidens Stone Circle, near Morvah, Cornwall

AFTER ARRIVAL AT JOHN O'GROATS.

John O'Groats is the last village in mainland Scotland but there's two more miles to go out to the lighthouse at Duncansby Head. Fine cliff scenery to the south with two stacks makes thiis very worthwhile. The actual most northerly point is Dunnet Head, 12 miles further west. On arrival at John O"Groats sign the register in the hotel there. You will find lots of cyclists have completed the trip from Land's End, but not so many people on foot, certainly less than 50 a year. There's souvenir shops of course, a food shop, restaurant, a youth hostel and a camp site. Particularly recommended is the day trip to Orkney, where a coach meets the ferry and takes you to the main places of interest on Orkney Mainland, including Kirkwall, Skara Brae, Langskaill House and the Ring of Brogar.

The nearest towns and railheads are Thurso, a hour's bus journey to the west, and Wick, a similar distance to the south. From them it's a five hour journey just to Inverness, eight hours or so to Glasgow or Edinburgh. For journeys to England either stay overnight somewhere further south in Scotland, or use the overnight Caledonian sleeper train leaving Inverness in the evening. This arrives in London around 8am, but a stop at Crewe around 5.30am allows connections through to most stations in England and Wales.

The Baddinsgill Reservoir and the Pentland Hills

LAND'S END TO BUDE

This 110m section mostly uses the coast path along the north side of Cornwall, but with inland sections to cut off headlands and see extra monuments. The coastal path is well signed in both directions and does not require a detailed route description here.

LAND'S END TO HAYLE. 24m, mostly coast path and inland bridleways. 5m on roads

The coast path heads north from the hotel at Land's End and then NE to a promontory fort known as Maen Castle, After just over a mile Sennen Cove is reached, which has a restaurant and cafe, and a beach that can be walked across for a mile instead of a path in sand dunes. After 4 miles the path goes slightly inland and just beyond the fifth mile drops to sea-level at Porth Nanven. Land's End youth hostel lies half a mile inland up the valley here, and the Kelynack bunkhouse and camp site another two thirds of a mile beyond up the same valley, although paths which may be rather overgrown allow cut-off routes to both hostels. Just north of the hostels lies the village of St Just, 1m off-route.

After a 300ft climb up the other side of the valley you pass a chimney and a triangulation point before arriving at Cape Cornwall, 6m from Land's End, where there's toilets and a building of doubtful age described as a chapel, but latterly used as a barn. After half a mile the path descends to cross a valley containing mine workings at Kenidjack, and the hamlet of Botallock with a pub and campsite lie to the NE, half a mile off route. Theres another set of mine workings further on before one walks through the mining complex of Levant. The mines here ran out far under the sea. In 1919 there was an accident here, killing 31 men when the machine to bring miners up from the depths collapsed. This mine is now a heritage site, parts of which can be visited (fee payable). Most of the mine ruins along this coast harmonise with the scenery, the spoil-heaps having long grassed over. An exception is the area just beyond the Levant mine where there is a more recent and unsightly mining complex in use from the 1960s until the 1990s.

Further north the path cuts just inland of the lighthouse at Pendeen and then descends to sea-level where there are stepping stones over a stream at Porteras Cove. A mile east of here take the path across the fields to MORVAH, where the church is mostly of 1820 but with a medieval tower. This marks the start of an inland section allowing southward views towards Mount's Bay from the road leaving the south side of B3306 a quarter of a mile east of Morvah. This route bypasses hostels, shops and campsites at St Ives and Carbis Bay, shortening the distance to Hayle and avoiding steep climbs and descents upon the coast path as it passes Zennor. At a road junction with what appears to be a fake modern quoit (burial chamber) turn right. At the cross-roads on Bosullow Common, a mile beyond Morvah, take the track heading NE signed Men-an-Tol. This monument, 13m from Land's End, is reached by a side track to the south and has a central stone with a circular hole in it and sighting stones forming a line (photo page 4).

Return to the main track and follow it past Men Seryfa (a standing stone). The path curves round to the right, heading for the Nine Maidens, a small but fine stone circle. If your path seems to be heading straight for the chimney at SW 455344, go back and take another path heading more easterly. From the stone circle take the narrow path through the heather to another engine-house with a chimney at SW 442348, keeping the patch of trees to your right. Take the track to the left just before arriving at the engine-house, and then keep left, joining a lane at SW 444348. Go left, and then left again. Before long there's a sign directling you up a track to the Bodrifty round-houses, which are the lower parts of a complex of Iron-Age huts recently conserved and opened to the public (free) with sign boards. Your route passes through the site and out the northern corner. If you're prepared to pay a fee and do an extra mile of road a diversion to the south is possible to see the English Heritage managed site of Chysauster (at SW 472350), which is a larger and better preserved group of Iron-Age houses similar to Bodrifty.

From Bodrifty follow the path NE to the road junction at SW452360, and take the road opposite heading east, Ignore the first left but go left in two thirds of a mile. This leads to a bridleway over to Amalveor with fine eastward views over St Ives Bay. From Almalveor take a delightful winding leafy lane beside a stream to Nantcledra. turn right for a few yards onto B3311 before taking another lane heading SE. After a quarter of a mile go left at a crossroads, and take a bridleway between fields on the right in a third of a mile after crossroads. The middle section may be muddy. It leads to a lane through modern houses down to the A30. Go down the pavement of this road past St Erth station, and over a roundabout onto the B3301 to Hayle, which is 24m from Land's End.

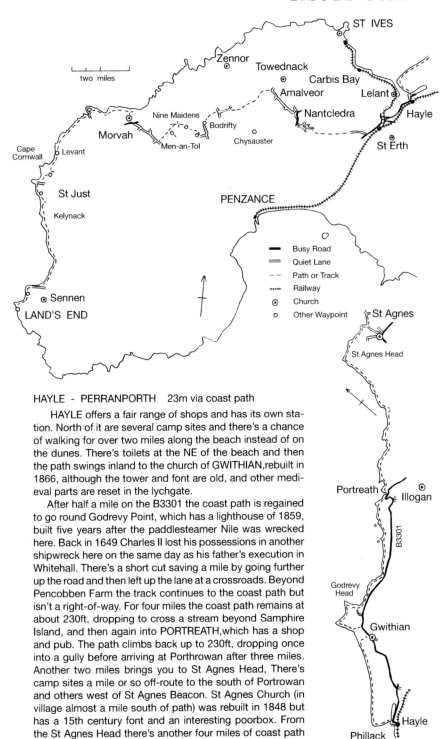

HAYLE - PERRANPORTH   23m via coast path

HAYLE offers a fair range of shops and has its own station. North of it are several camp sites and there's a chance of walking for over two miles along the beach instead of on the dunes. There's toilets at the NE of the beach and then the path swings inland to the church of GWITHIAN,rebuilt in 1866, although the tower and font are old, and other medieval parts are reset in the lychgate.

After half a mile on the B3301 the coast path is regained to go round Godrevy Point, which has a lighthouse of 1859, built five years after the paddlesteamer Nile was wrecked here. Back in 1649 Charles II lost his possessions in another shipwreck here on the same day as his father's execution in Whitehall. There's a short cut saving a mile by going further up the road and then left up the lane at a crossroads. Beyond Pencobben Farm the track continues to the coast path but isn't a right-of-way. For four miles the coast path remains at about 230ft, dropping to cross a stream beyond Samphire Island, and then again into PORTREATH,which has a shop and pub. The path climbs back up to 230ft, dropping once into a gully before arriving at Porthrowan after three miles. Another two miles brings you to St Agnes Head, There's camp sites a mile or so off-route to the south of Portrowan and others west of St Agnes Beacon. St Agnes Church (in village almost a mile south of path) was rebuilt in 1848 but has a 15th century font and an interesting poorbox. From the St Agnes Head there's another four miles of coast path to PERRANPORTH, 47m from Land's End which has a range of shops and places to stay, plus a youth hostel.

PERRANPORTH TO NEWQUAY   7m, using 5m of roads and tidal bridge over Gannel.

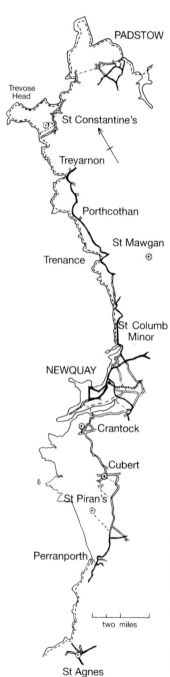

From the centre of Perranporth follow B3285 round a bend over a stream and then take a cut-off path up the hillside. The B-road swings to the SE shortly after you rejoin it but the coastal path is reached by going along the minor road to the NE for a mile. There's free access onto the dunes known as Penhale Sands so you can make a diversion to see the sand-covered remains of St Piran's Church and medieval cross both located a quarter of a mile east of the tall modern wooden cross, but there's no continuous coastal path here because of the army camp north of the huge holiday camp. From the road the path, rather poorly defined, runs for half a mile until it crosses a stream and then turns left out bto the coast. Cut the corner off by going straight on up to CUBERT. Turn right at a road, then right again into a housing estate to pick up a path running through the churchyard. There's toilets hidden beside a house east of church (sign invisible from churchyard), and there's a shop and post office. Trebellan camp-site lies to the south (at SW 790572). Cubert Church is a cruciform building mostly of c1300 but the tower and broach-spire are of 1852. The font is 13th century and the pulpits are made up of old parts. There is a 7th century stone on the tower.

From Cubert follow the roads northwards to CRANTOCK, which has toilets, and shops, plus two pubs. Parts of the cruciform church are Norman, but the chancel and its chapels are 14th century, the tower is 15th century and the screen dates mostly from a restoration of 1890. If the tide is in its a two and half miler walk round the estuary called the Gannel to the centre of NEWQUAY. If the tide is out use the road running NE out of Crantock past a building using a former ship's figurehead as a lintel on the right, This leads down to a small inlet opposite where there is a bridge over the stream covered at high tide. Use the path going east along the north side of the Gannel until you reach a road climbing the hill northwards. Follow the line of this into the west end of Newquay, coming out by the bus station, behind which is the main street and most of the shops. Newquay is 54m from Land's End via the bridge over the Gannel and offers all the range of shops and services you are likely to need, including a camping and outdoor shop at SW 814618, just to the west of the terminal station of a branch railway line which comes over from the main line at Par.

You can buy a tide timetable at Cubert and if the tide's going to be in you could bypass Crantock and use the paths through Carevick Farm (SW 795588- almost worth it alone for the sight of a sign actually welcoming walkers!) Then use the lanes to Trevemper to head out to the Morrisons supermarket at SW 825601, From here you can use a road heading NW and then take a path heading north over the railway to bypass the centre of Newquay. This cuts off some of the road walking needed to get out off the centre of Newquay.

Tidal bridge over the Gannel, south of Newquay

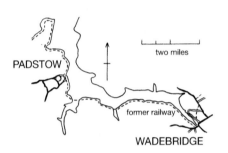

Font in Crantock Church

NEWQUAY TO WADEBRIDGE   22m. Coastal paths, 5m on old railway, 3m on roads.

The first mile or so beyond Newquay town centre is mostly on roads until you reach coastal paths again at Whipsidery. There's then a` short cut, bypassing the promontory fort of Trevelgue Head. The path descends to sea-level at Watergate Bay, which has hotels, toilets and a kiosk, and again at Trenance where there's remains of a Dark Age settlement on the other (east) side of B3276. If the tide is out a short-cut is possible across Porthcothan beach, missing out the toilets. After another mile there's another fort, known as Redcliffe, and then another half a mile brings you to Treyarnon youth hostel. Cut off Trevose Head and its lighthouse of 1847 by taking the road inland at the south end of Constantine Bay. Take a short path left opposite the toilets through to the drive of Les Nook Chalets and keep left on the path before the chalets. Join the road heading NE beside a golf course, across which there's a possible diversion to see the little that's not buried in dunes of St Constantine's Church. Just north of the church is something more interesting, ruins of a vaulted well chapel now covered by a modern shelter. A bit further on a path cuts off a corner of the road and allows a glimpse of the north side of the old house of Harlyn, appearing late 18th century on this side, but with medieval work on the south side. Take a second path opposite when you rejoin the road and then after a short section on a lane, you can rejoin the coast path as far as Trevone. After crossing the stream take the lane heading NE and then turn right along the track (actually a byway open to all traffic) passing along the south side of Porthmissen Farm. This cuts off Stepper Point, coming out at a cross-roads where the road opposite leads down into PAD-STOW. The town has a fair range of shops and places to stay, and Prideaux Place, a late 16th century E-plan house, is open to the public. Parts of the church are 13th century but the aisles are 14th century and have good wagon roofs. There are old benches, a fine font and several monuments of interest, whilst there is a Saxon cross-shaft outside.

Follow the shore south of the town and eventually you'll come to the start of the 5 mile section of the Camel Trail into Wadebridge. Its easy walking along a former railway line opened in 1899 with good views of the estuary. Once on this section there's no places to stay or camp before reraching the centre of WADEBRIDGE, 76 miles from Land's End. Wadebridge has a reasonable range of shops and places to stay, toilets, and hourly buses through to Bodmin and Bodmin Road station.

WADEBRIDGE TO TINTAGEL   14m. 9m inland section, half on roads, then coast path.

Cross the 17-arch bridge over the River Camel at Wadebridge which dates from c1468, but widened in 1847 and 1962. John Leland claimed the piers were sunk into the river bed on sacks of wool. Follow A39 round to the left, then take a track on the left off the first corner, off which after a few yards is a path on the right. After half a mile turn right onto a track, then left to cut through to the B3314, which is followed northwards for a quarter of a mile over a stream and past a lane on the right before taking a path on the right through the fields which comes out on a road just SE of Chapel Amble. Turn left into the village and turn right towards St Kew. Pass a crossroads and three other roads off to the left, with a medieval cross-shaft by one of the junctions, and then take a nice path on the right for the last half mile into ST KEW. The church here has good stained glass dated 1467. The layout is typical of that period in Cornwall, an aisled parallellagram of granite with a west tower with buttresses set back from the corners. The wagon-roofs, font, south door, pulpit, and Royal Arms of 1661 are all of interest. There is also a 6th or 7th century ogham stone with a script of straight lines across one edge.

Go through the churchyard and follow a lane northwards for over a mile to cross over B3267 and then turn right onto B3314 at Pendoggett, where there's a pub. There are paths to the NW from Pendoggett to link with the coast path again at Port Gaverne, just east of the village of Port Isaac, but this is a long way round, the paths are likely to be overgrown, and going that way involves a 400ft climb and then descending to sea-level again. Thus it's easier to do a mile and a quarter along B3314 heading NE past the over-grown earthworks of the fort of Tregeare Rounds. Turn left at a cross-roads, and down the track past Hendra Farm leading to a path to the coast path at Barret's Zawn. Much of the next five mile section to Tintagel is at around 300ft above the sea, but there are descents to cross two streams near Barret's Zawn, and further on there's two more, on either side of Dennis Point. Your refreshments in Tintagel will have been well earned.

Full of tourists in summer, and with several quaint old buildings, such as the Old Post Office, TINTAGEL is 90m from Land's End, and has several shops, restaurants, pubs and places to stay. Much of the cruciform church lying alone west of the village is Norman, with several windows of that period and the 13th century, whilst the north porch is 14th century, and there is a west tower of uncertain date. A fine font, a rood screen, a small brass of a female of c1430, and a Roman milestone are included in the features of interest inside. The very ruined castle is administered by English Heritage (entrance fee payable). It was built by Henry III's brother Richard, Earl of Cornwall in the mid 13th century and improved a century later by Edward III's eldest son Edward the Black Prince, although military campaigns on the continent and duties at court would have prevented either of these lords from paying more than occasional brief visits to Tintagel. The spactacularly placed ruins lie on either side of a collapsed causeway over to a headland (The Island) upon which have been found huts going back to c500, hence the Arthurian legends associated with this place.

Tintagel Castle

Tintagel Church

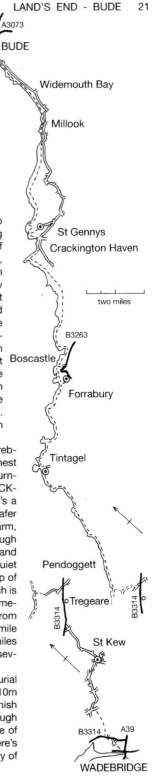

TINTAGEL TO BUDE 20m by coast path.
5m or more of road alternatives in bad weather.

Four miles of dramatic cliff-top path with one drop into the Rocky Valley (where there's a campsite) bring you over a set of medieval strip lychetts to the church of FORRABURY, partly Norman, with a font of that period, a tower of 1750 and a north aisle of 1867. The church serves the village of BOSCASTLE in the valley below it. The harbour area, where the youth hostel, witchcraft museum and other touristy places are, was devastated by flash flooding a few years ago. One of the two stone jetties was destroyed by a mine in WW2. Nothing remains of the castle of the Botreaux family from which the place takes its name. The only camp site here is at Trebyle Farm (SX 119921). Rather than walking a mile up B3263 to get to it, use the delightful path through woods on the north side of the River Valency for a mile and then climb the steep zig-zag lane up from Newmills. However you will miss the 120ft high waterfall down onto the beach at Pentargon if you make this detour.

Otherwise stay on the coast path, which north of Trebyle Farm climbs to 247m as it goes over High Cliff (highest point on the whole SW peninsular coast path) before turning sharrply east at Cambreak and descending to CRACKINGTON HAVEN, 101m from Land's End, where there's a hotel and public toilets. Under windy conditions its safer to follow the lane north for over a mile from Newton Farm, and then drop down to the right to follow a path through a wooded valley into Crackington Haven. A lot of up and down on the coast path is avoided by using the arc of quiet lanes east of the church of ST GENNYS, itself at the top of a steep 430ft climb from Crackington Haven. The church is partly Norman, with a font of that date, and partly late medieval, although the tower top is early 20th century. From the roads you can rejoin the cliff path two thirds of a mile before the descent to MiLLOOK. Its then another 2 miles to the toilets at WIDEMOUTH BAY, south of which lie several campsites.

A mile further on the path skirts a tumulus or burial mound, and another two miles brings you to BUDE, 110m fron Land's End. Its one of the least attractive Cornish resorts, and the church dates only from 1835, although the vicarage may be 15th century. There is a fair range of shops, restaurants, pubs, a chippy, toilets, etc, and there's direct buses to Exeter St Davids Station. There's plenty of B&Bs and two camp-sites.

BUDE TO MINEHEAD

74m. Three sections of dramatic but tough cliff top path for start, finish and middle. Inland cut-offs involve some long road sections. One easy section on old railway trackbed.

BUDE TO BIDEFORD 27m. 14m of roads, rest most very steep coast path sections..

North of Bude there's a lot of steep climbs and descents on the coast path, in fact there's 7000ft of climb on the 32 miles of coast path before you turn off inland for a final three miles mostly on roads into Bideford. About half of the climbs and descents are on steps, so although the scenery is fantastic with amazing folded rock formations and Clovelly is really lovely, you'll have to work very hard to see it all. The YHA has recently closed the hostel at Elmscott but there's places to stay, plus pubs and shops, in Hartland and Clovelly. There's a hotel at Hartland Quay, toilets just east of Hartland Church, and a refreshment kiosk by the car-park SE of Hartland Point. Those arriving on foot along the coast path can get into Clovelly free instead of paying to go through visitor centre from the car park, so don't be tempted to access Clovelly from the main roads to the SW.

The route described below offers a much easier alternative using several miles of roads which are quiet, but aren't particularly pretty, nor do they have fine views. If you walk via Hartland Point add 7 miles to your total and allow 3300ft of extra climbing (lots of steps!) to the 1000ft of climb on the road route between Morwenstow Church and rejoining the coast path just east of Bucks Mills. From Morwenstow just to Clovelly along the coast path represents a good day's walk. Note that beyond Hartland Point there's a two mile flattish section east of Titchberry which is a fairly new path along the edges of fields without much in the way of a seaward view. Note also you can save 300ft of climb on the half mile section immediately after crossing into Devon by walking along a beach to Welcome Mouth. However there's slippery rocks to negotiate, and an injury caused by a fall could lead to stranding and drowning by the tide, so be careful.

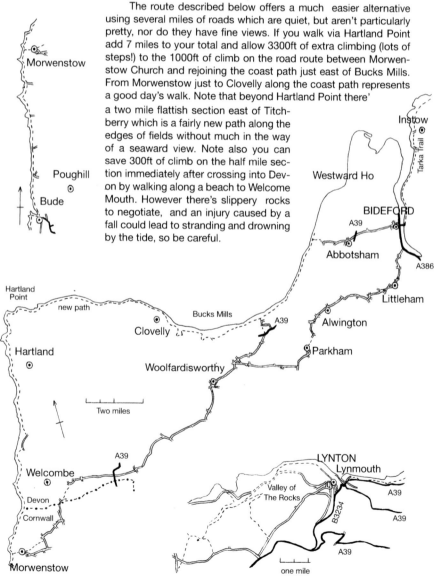

The coast path climbs gradually out of Bude, goes beside a tumulus at Menachurch Point (there's a couple of others earlier), and drops to sea-level at Sandy Mouth, again at Combe (where there's toilets), and twice more before MORWENSTOW, which is 7m from Bude. The National Trust own R.S.Hawker's vicarage, and his tiny wooden hut below the coast path is their smallest property. There's a toilet with a tap and sink behind the parish church and a pub (the Bush Inn) which allows backpackers to camp. Much of the church and some of its furnishings (eg bench-ends) are 16th century, but there's a Norman north arcade surmounted by animal heads, east of which are two 13th century arches, and the fine south doorway and the font are also Norman work.

The path leading ENE across a valley from the church is not easy to follow so its best to take the road east from the pub, turn left after half a mile, and then right at a staggered cross-roads after a third of a mile. Go over a cross-roads and in Gooseham turn left at a T-junction down to Gooseham Mill, where there's a bridge over Marshland Water, marking the boundary between Cornwall and Devon, 9m from Bude. Take a path on the right through woods after a short distance. When the path divides keep left to follow the west side of a tributary stream up onto a farm lane. Turn right when the farm lane meets other roads at a cross, right again at a T-junction, and over a crossroads at the 190m contour. You'll pass a campsite just before crossing over A39 at Welcombe Cross. You'll arrive at the SW corner of the square of roads at Meldon village, and you leave from the NE corner, still heading east. The road bends and passes plantations. Turn right a mile from Meldon, then left. Pass two more plantations, go round a sharp bend where the Gorrel Farm track comes in from the right, go over a crossroads and then in another mile reach WOOLFARDISWORTHY (often shortened to Woolsery), 8m from the county boundary and 17m from Bude. There's a post-office-cum-shop, a pub, and a fine old church with Norman work in the south transept, south doorway and font, The late medieval west tower has angle-buttresses and a polygonal stair turret on one side.

Ffrom Woolfardisworthy take the road leading east from the south side of the church for a mile to the crossroads at Cranford. If you like old churches turn east here and use mostly quiet roads via Parkham, Alwington, and Littleham. This route to Bideford is only slightly longer than going back on the coast path, and the climbs are easier, but it ends with a fifteen minute walk northwards along A386 to Bideford. To reach the coast path cross over at Cranford, immediately turn right, go over a crossroads, and, after a mile, turn right onto A39 for a short way until there's a path on the left. It becomes a track beyond a house. At a road turn left round a corner, and then there's access to the coast path from the next corner. You'll drop to sea-level again after a mile at Peppercombe. There's no sign of the castle marked on the map. Before turning inland (at SS 406272) after another 2.5 miles there's four steep climbs, the last on them a 300ft rise up from a short section of stony beach after stepping stones over a stream. The path inland brings you round the north and east of Greencliff and onto a corner of a road. Head left (east), keep left in half a mile, and left again to reach the church of ABBOTSHAM, a cruciform 13th century building with a tower on the north side, a Norman font and 15th or 16th century bench ends. Fork right just after the church to go under the A39 and reach BIDEFORD, 137m from Land'd End. An attractiive and steeply sloping town of 13,000 inhabitants offering all services, but lacking buildings of individual importance, Bideford was once an important port, trading in fish and tobacco. The old parish church west of the bridge was rebuilt in 1862 except for the late medieval tower, but it has a Norman font and the monuments include a tomb of Sir Thomas Grenville, d1513.

BIDEFORD - BARNSTAPLE 9 easy miles on railway trackbed, a tarmaced cycle route.

Cross the Torridge estuary on the 24 arch bridge, a 15th century structure, modified in 1638 and widened in 1865. The coast path joins the cycle track known as the Tarka Trail all the way to where the railway remains open (towards Exeter) south of Barnstaple station. A frequent bus service connects Bideford with Barnstaple station. East of Instow is a youth hostel, and north of the village, 4m along the trail, is a picnic place, but there's nowhere else to stay or camp between Bideford and the other side of the town centre of Barnstaple, which lies half a mile east of station, over an impressive bridge which is 13th century in origin, although its been widened and rebuilt to the point where you'd have to pass underneath it to see any medieval arches now.

BARNSTAPLE TO LYNTON 7m on paths and 11m on roads

BARNSTAPLE lies 146m from Land's End and offers all services. With 20,000 inhabitants it's the largest English town whose main street lies on your route. Only a mound in a park remains of the castle of Judhael of Totnes and nothing of the town walls. Both were reported ruinous by Leland in the 1530s. Almshouses are the main relic of the period when Barnstaple was a major port in the 16th and 17th centuries. The church is partly late medieval and partly Victorian, but has a 12th cedntury south transeptal tower with lead-covered 14th century broach-spire which has become rather twisted, and selection of monuments. In the secluded churchyard is a 14th century chantry chapel later used as a school, now a museum.

There's a second old church closeby at PILTON just over the Yeo, reached by turning right at the end of Barnstaple High St, and heading down Pilton Causeway. The church is reached through mock-Tudor almshouses of 1849 and is late medieval on the south side but earlier on the north, where there are signs of the former cloister of a Benedictine priory, and a transeptal tower rebuilt in the 1690s and again in the 1840s. Inside are two large monuments to members of the Chichester family and fine late medieval furnishings, including a stone pulpite with a later tester. Bull House to the SW was either the prior's lodging or the priory guest-house, built in the 15th century.

Take the lane NE from here, to start of a cut-off avoiding the long detour of coast path through Braunton, Woolacombe, Ilfracombe and Combe Martin. After a third of a mile take the path on the left. After half a mile it joins a short lane leading to B3230, which is followed northwards for a quarter of a mile before taking a lane on the right leading to Hartpiece. Beyond the farm a path climbs up over South Hill, and along the south side of some woods. Turn left along A 39 for a quarter of a mile and then take the lane on the right to SHIRWELL, where the church is a cruciform 13th century building with several monuments in the 14th century chancel, A late medieval aisle and porch have been added west of the south transeptal tower. Go east from Shirwell and keep left after a stream. Turn left after another stream and then immediate go straight over up the hill at the crossing of roads at tracks at Loxhore Cott. Go left at the top and ignore the lane left up to Loxhore Church unless you are keen enough to make a half mile diversion to see the lovely interiror with an unusual arcade of wood.

The road then climbs up onto a ridge almost 270m up. Two miles beyond the turning to Loxhore Church tracks along the NW side of Westlandpound Reservoir offer a brief alternative to road walking, and there's picnic tables. Where the lane meets A399, almost 300m up at SS 650429, take the path opposite the lane for a mile until it meets A39. Opposite the path is a lane going down into PARRACOMBE on the NW flank of Exmoor. East of the lane is a spur made into the motte and bailey earthworks of Holwell Castle, Parracombe has a pub and shop, and there's toilets with taps and siinks on the playing fields. A third of a mile further east lies the redundant old church, 13th and 15th century with a superb set of rustic furnishings.

The A39 arcs around to the east of Parracombe and unfortunately you need to rejoin it for an uphill third of a mile before there's a path on the left. This goes under a recently restored section of the old narrow guage railway between Infracombe and Lynton. On Martinhoe Common turn left down a lane for a very short distance before there's another path on the right. It crosses another land and descends to cross a stream at Croscombe Barton. You then join a track headsing NE through woodland. This turns into a path which leads through the spectacular Valley of the Rocks to Lynton.

LYNTON

Valley of Rocks

two miles

Parracombe

A39

Holwell Castle

A339

Kentisbury

East Down

Loxore

Shirwell

A39

Pilton

Ashford

BARNSTAPLE

Fremington

Tarka Trail

LYNTON - MINEHEAD   20m, mostly on coast path..

MINEHEAD

A39

two miles

Selworthy
⊙

Lynch
A39
⊙ Porlock

Porlock Weir

Culbone ⊙

Oare
⊙ Somerset

Devon
A39

Countisbury
⊙

Lynmouth

LYNTON
See page 22

LYNTON lies 164 from Land's End and offers all services. To the south of the youth hostel are two campsites. Only a Norman font and the tower of the church have survived the additions and rebuildings of the 1860s, 1890s and 1905 Unless you are going to cheat by going down on the cliff railway built in 1890, the only access between the bustling town of Lynton and the adjoining pretty village of Lynmouth far below it is down the pavement of the steep B3234. Originally a fishing village, and noted as the scene of a disasterous flood in August 1952, when a terrible storm swelled the East and West Lyn rivers, Lynmouth is tourist place, full of souvenir shops and cafes. Buy an icecream or drink in readiness for the uphill slog climbing 1000ft in a mile and a half up to the church of COUNTISBURY, rebuilt in 1796, 1835 and 1845, near which is a pub called the Blue Ball. If its sunny you'll be grateful the first half, at least, is through woodland. Going out to Foreland Point means an extra climb out of Coddow Comb afterwards so from the church keep on the path further inland parallel to A39 until you can turn left onto a track descending the east flank of Coddow Comb. The path stays high up, passes through woodland, crosses the valleys of two streams before swinging inland in woodland to cross the deeper valley of a stream marking the boundary between Devon and Somerset, 170m from L.E. and a third of a mile north of the toilets at County Gate on the A39, south of which is a very steep drop to the East Lyn River. On a hilltop on the Devon side was a Roman signal station, built to keep an eye on the Welsh.

A climb up past East Yenworthy Farm brings the path back up to the 1000ft level. It eventually drops after a couple of miles to reach the tiny and delightful old church at CULBONE, accompanied only by two houses. Another mile and a half, still on a windy woodland path high above the sea, brings you to a descent to PORLOCK WEIR, where there's a small harbour with toilets and a pub (the Ship). Along B3225 its then two miles to PORLOCK but you can cut out nearly half of the road walking by taking first the coast path on the left after a third of a mile, and then another path to the right, leading eventually to a track back to the road, or you can bypass Porlock by hugging the coast, going past the bird sanctuary on Porlock Marsh, and not turning inland until Bossington, near Lynch. Lying astride A39, Porlock has several shops and toilets and the church is of various periods with a shingled spire on the 13th century tower, and a splendid 15th century monument to the Harrington family set under the 14th century south arcade.   .

When A39 turns sharply south 400yards east of the church take the lane to LYNCH, which has a medieval chapel. Take bridleway up the hill through woodland almost opposite the old chapel, climbing 300m onto Selworthy Beacon in just over a mile. The coast path remains on a high ridge until the descent into Minehead. There a possible diversion to see the minmal remains of the Burgundy Chapel. Lying 184m from Land's End and a population of 11,000, MINEHEAD offers all services, a youth hostel somewhat to the south, and has a station at the end of a steam railway now running to Bishop's Lydiard, although the rails survive to Taunton The old church up to the SW is mostly late medieval with a rood screen, font and several monuments all of that period and a later pulpit. The old hurch, harbour, station and the main shopping centre with a statue of Queen Anne dating from 1719 in Willington Square all lie quite separate from each other.

MINEHEAD TO CHEPSTOW

Very mixed 81m. Tracks over two high heaths, roads &
paths across low level marshes, two urban areas, two
spectacular bridges, many interesting old churches.

MINEHEAD - CLEEVE 3m on roads & 5m on paths

From the centre of Minehead walk along the pavement of A39 to Alcombe and then take the back road
to Dunster. Footpaths only really make a viable alternative here if you are staying at Minehead Youth Hostel on heathland a mile south of the town. Stock up
in Minehead since the shops in DUNSTER offer little
apart from souvenirs, fudge and icrecream. They lie in
a pretty wide street with an octagonal market cross of
1589. The cruciform church lying further SW is mostly
a late medieval building which once served a Benedictine priory. Part of a Norman west doorway remains,
and there are many effigies and other monuments, plus
old screens. On an isolated hill to the south is the castle, mostly now a 16th, 17th and 19th century stately
home in National Trust care. Originally a Mohun seat, it
was sold to the Luttrells in 1376. The castle withstood
sieges in 1139, 1642, 1643 and 1645-6, after which the
defences were removed except for the 13th century inner gateway and the 15th century outer gateway containing a court room on the top floor.

Your route out to the south passes an old mill and
goes over the Gallox clapper bridge. Just to the south
you'll pick up the signs of the Macmillan Way. After
climbing onto a ridge and turning left the way crosses
through an Iron Age fort known as Bat's Castle. The
way then heads east over Aller Hill and Withycombe Hill
to WITHYCOMBE, 5m from Minehead. The church here
contains two medieval effigies and an old screen. It has
a porch-tower on the south side, and is mostly 13th
and 14th century, a rarity in Somerset, where churches
are mostly later medieval, i.e. 15th - 16th century.

Take a road eastwards out of Withycombe and
follow the path heading SE just after a lane goes off
to the south. A bush marks the bearing of the second gateway you need to go through. The path goes
through woods, over the Pill River, turns a corner at
Escott Farm and then runs to a road junction, where
you turn left, heading east. The Macmillan Way soon
heads off right across a field but stay on the road, and
go over a crossroads onto a farm track. The path off to
the right isn't obvious so follow the track as it zig-zags
down through Hungerford Farm, not a right of way, but
there didn't seem to be a problem. Turn left on a road
to reach the Cistercian Abbey of CLEEVE, founded in
1198, now in the custody of English Heritage (toilets).
The 13th century cloistral ranges are unusually well
preserved, the monks' dormitory still being roofed (a
great rarity in Britain), with a vaulted undercroft and the
chapter house below. There are exhibitions in the south
range which originally contained the refectory but was
later made into a house, hence the survival of the roof.
However, not much now remains of the church on the
north side of the cloister.

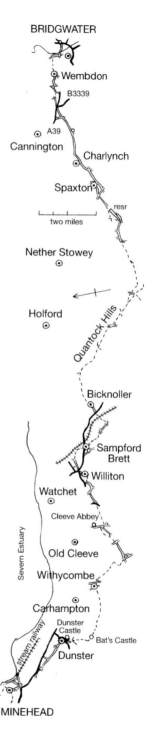

CLEEVE ABBEY - BRIDGWATER   15m mostly on paths, plus 5m mostly roads.

From the abbey go back down the road southwards past the White Horse pub (B&B), and turn left onto the Macmillan Way again. After half a mile the way sweeps south just west of Bardon Farm, but its easier to follow another path round the farm and down its lane. Cross over B3190 onto a quiet lane, turn right, ignore a road off to the right but then turn right down a farm track just before reaching A39. The right of way here is in the process of being legally diverted away from the stables and buildings, and leads over a stream onto a road past the old (but mostly rebuilt) parish church of WILLITON.
As you follow A39 for a quarter of a mile along in Williton you'll pass several shops, and there's toilets on the car park on the right just before A39 turns east. A path heading south from A39 beside playing fields leads to a road. Turn left. Ignore the path beside a stream on the left. Instead turn right and then left across a field to reach a green lane to SAMPFORD BRETT, 12m from Minehead, where the church has a 13th century north transept and a 14th century south transeptal tower, although much of the rest is of 1835. Go down a lane from the church, to reach a path through to a green lane heading SE to a road. Turn left, and immediately left again, heading NE. Soon after crossing Doniford Brook take the path on the right leading to a railway level crossing and to A358. Turn right on the main road for a short distance, then left into Bicknoller.
    BICKNOLLER is 14m from Minehead and has a typical Somerset late medieval church with a fine south porch,and a rood screen. At the northern apex of the tiny triangle of roads north of the church there's a cross-roads, the Macmillan Way following a stony track heading NE then east onto the summit of the Quantock Hills. Follow the main path heading SE over Black Ball Hill, over the road at Crowcombe Park Gate, and down to the Triscombe Stone, where a road goes off left. Take the track right off the road (you can in fact use a path to cut off the corner where the stone is) and follow it through Quantock Forest round the head of Cockercombe, to emerge after a mile to follow the southern edge of the forest. Join a road heading east. Ignore two roads on the left, and take a path alongside the north edge of Hawkridge Reservoir. At a crossing of paths south of some woodland turn right to continue along above the reservoir. This path zigzags over the stream coming out of the reservoir and leads to a lane past Ebsley Farm. Go over a crossroads to reach SPAXTON, 23m from Minehead.
    Turn right by the church, which is mostly late medieval with older parts and contains two effigies. Turn left and then in half a mile left again and after another half a mile there's an option of a small detour to see the Norman (but over-restored) church of CHAR-LYNCH. A mile further on the road passes Gothelney Hall, dating from c1500. The lane leads to where A39 and B3339 converge. Cross over both, taking a lane heading east, and continue east on a path when the lane goes north. Turn right then left at the path junctions (this looks like a crossroads on the Landranger map but isn't), turn left onto a lane, fork right, go round a bend and turn left. At the end this lane zigzags to reach the church of WEMBDON, mostly a rebuild of the 1860s. A track running east to the south of the church becomes a path, although a new estate is being built here. Cross over a road to gain the path running south alongside the west bank of the River

East range of Cleeve Abbey

Parrett towards the centre of BRIDGWATER, 28m from Minehead, 212m from Land's End. It offers all services, although your route over a bridge at ST 300374 bypasses the town centre, beyond which is the large cruciform church of St Mary with a tall spire on the 14th century central tower. The rest is mostly 15th and 19th century, and there old screens and 17th century monuments. There are good 18th century houses in Castle Street and King's Square, which lie on the site of an early 13th century castle built by William Brewer but later held by the Mortimers and then the Crown. Most of it was destroyed after capture by Parliamentary troops in 1645, but immediately north of the Watergate Hotel is a section of wall facing the river containing the gateway after which the hotel is named.

BRIDGWATER - CHEDDAR   19m. 10m of roads and 9m of easy, flat paths

If you don't need to shop in Bridgwater you can cross the River Parret on the bridge at ST 300374, head east to a roundabout and then walk along a pavement beside A39 for a mile and a half, taking the second lane on nthe right after crossing the M5. After a third of a mile take the path across the fields and a bridge over King's Sedgemoor Drain into BAWDRIP, 3m from Bridgwater. The nave and north transept of the church are 14th century but the central tower, chancel and south transept are 13th century. A path along the north side of the former railway line leads to a camp-site at the junction of B3141 and A39. Go a short distance east on A39 and then take a path cutting diagonally across fields to a lane just south of the church at COSSINGTON. This building is mostly 15th century with a few older bits. There's an effigy near the porch and brasses of c1530 on the chancel floor.

Take the lane leading NE out of Cossington. There's a crossroads to go over and a double bend before reaching a bridge over the Huntspill River. Turn right and then follow a track round to the left. When it turns right carry straight on along a path which joins a lane just east of where it crosses the Cripps River. Turn right, and then after two thirds of a mile turn left over the River Brue. After a mile turn right to Yarrow. After following a drain for a third of a mile a path allows a short-cut over to the church at MARK, 11 miles from Bridgwater. This is a fine 15th century building with a tall west tower and splendid north porch. The font, pulpit, rood-screen and a few bits of stained glass are also 15th or 16th century. There's also a shop and a pub in the village.

Follow B3139 east from Mark church, turning left after a third of a mile. About a mile and a half from the church fork right a short distance to pick up a path on the west side of a drain. After a short distance cross the drain and pick up a track zig-zagging through to STONE ALLERTON. Follow the lanes zig-zagging through the village and beyond out to the NE to reach the church at WEARE, 16m from Bridgwater. It has a 15th century tower, a small brass of c1500, and a Norman font, but was much altered in 1846, when a north aisle was added. A short track leading east just south of the church gives access to a path over to Cradle Bridge. Just before the next bridge, over Cheddar Yeo, turn right and follow the river for a quarter of a mile before crossing it onto a good track which goes round the south side of Cheddar Reservoir and into the west end of CHEDDAR village. Your route uses A371 for a short distance before going left, then right, then left up Upper North Lane beside the Baptist Church, This brings you to the start of a good path leading up over the Mendips from ST 457542. Lying further east from the direct route are the famous limestone Cheddar Gorge with its caves once inhabited by prehistoric men, the youth hostel, and the village centre with several shops, a medieval market cross, and the fine 14h and 15th century church with old roofs, an unusually lofty west tower, lots of old furnishings, stained glass, and two brasses.

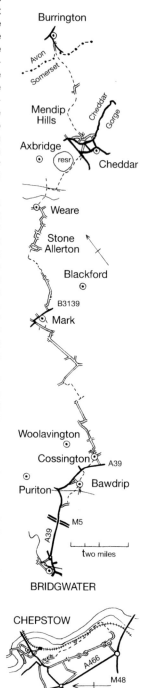

CHEDDAR - CLIFTON   17m. Roads 3m in total. Very varied paths. One long climb.

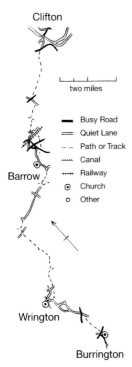

Clifton

two miles

■ Busy Road
= Quiet Lane
- - Path or Track
⌣⌣⌣ Canal
+++ Railway
⊙ Church
○ Other

Barrow

Wrington

Burrington

From Cheddar the path climbs steeply at first, and then becomes a wider and gentler track. It joins just a short section of road between a group of barrows before a path beside Tyning's Farm leads steeply up to the 1000ft high summit of this part of the Mendip Hills, 2m from Cheddar. Cross over two paths and keep heading north until the path joins a track down a valley and eventually bends right to join B3134 a third of a mile north of where there's a carpark with toilets. From here the B3134 leads south and then east into Burrington Combe, a smaller verson of Cheddar Grorge, with several caves inhabited in prehistoric times, whilst on the hill opposite the carpark is an Iron Age fort.

Go north on the B3134 a short distance before taking a short path over to the church at BURRINGTON. This is another fine Somerset late medieval church with good old roofs and a south porch, although the short west tower is earlier. Go along the north side of the church and turn left onto a vlane up to A368, then take the bridleway opposite up to Havyatt Green. Expect a bit of mud along the middle section of this, but its better than the invisible path running parallel not far to the west. Turn left onto a lane, cross over A38 and take the lanes up to Wrington, having forked right and gone past Mill Farm on the quieter of two alternative lanes. WRINGTON has a very fine mostly late-medieval church with a very lofty west tower but your route bypasses it, keeping a third of a mile to the east and at ST 472625 taking a path heading almost east and going north from the junction of paths at ST 475627. Turn left along a lane to a crossroads and then go right onto a track heading along the east side of Prestow Wood. After half a mile take the left fork on a track which becomes a bridleway heading north through woodland on the east side of Wrington Warren.

Turn right onto a lane at The Batch, then left onto a path, only to turn right after a short distance. This feeds through to a track which becomes a lane. Go over a crossroads and when the track ends at a gate turn left on a path. Before long, on a short open heath between two sections of woodland there's a sort of bent cross of paths. Cross over, but also head off to the right to meet a lane at ST 516678. Take the left fork and then in quarter of a mile cross over tracks leading off to Berrow Court on one side and Home Farm on the other. Berrow Court is a Jacobean house with formal gardens on the site of a Benedictine nunnery. The church beside it was rebuilt in 1889, but contains two 17th century monuments. Very shortly after crossing the track to the church there's a path off on the right. It leads across two fields and onto a curving track up to several houses. When the track reaches B3130 go just a few yards to the right before finding a stile into the field on the left. The opposite fence, bounding a stream, has lots of pallets along it and you'll need to look carefully to find the bridge. The path then skirts a field, crosses the track up to Redwood Farm and goes beside the stream again in a culvert to go under A370. It joins a track which crosses the railway east of Cambridge Batch. Turn right for a short distance, then left for a fifth of a mile until there's a path around the flank of Ashton Hill. After half a mile go left on a track for a short way before the path continues above the north side of Long Ashton. Ther's another bit where you turn left onto a track for a short way befolre the path continues. It climbs through woods and out to a road. Turn left, cross over B3128 and pick up a woodland track along the south side of a quarry which leads through to the open parkland of Ashton Court, a hopuse extended in 1635, 1805 and 1885 from a 15th century core by the Smyth family, Bristol merchants. Follow through to the gatehouse of 1885, and go down the road opposite to reach the CLIFTON SUSPENSION BRIDGE over the Avon.

CLIFTON - CHEPSTOW   17m, mostly by varied and surprisingly pleasant paths.

Although you've pentrated deep into Bristol suburbia, and will be amongst it for the next five miles north from the bridge, in total only about of a fifth of it really has the atmosphere of suburbia and the rest appears as attractive parkland walking. The city centre offering all services lies almost 2m off-route to the east of the bridge, and Temple Meads station is still further away to the SE, although there are other local stations closer to the Clifton bridge. Henry VIII made the former Augustinian abbey church with a very fine 14th century choir into a cathedral in 1540, and it was given a new nave in 1868 - 88. Much of the claustral ranges still survive, including a vaulted Norman chapter house. Between it and Temple Meads lies one of England's most magnificent medieval parish churches, that of St Mary Redcliffe. It is stone vaulted throughout, has transepts with east and west aisles, and a rare hexagonal porch. It lay outside the city walls, of which just one gateway remains beside the church of St John the Baptist. Despite the damage caused by wartime bombing, several other old churches also survive, one of them originally having a very rare circular nave. Of the important royal castle demolished by an order of Parliament in 1655 there remain just porches from the domestic apartments, footings of the huge keep, and a few other minor fragments. Other attractions include the quayside and early steamship SS Great Britain, west of which, one mile off route at ST 574722, is a campsite, although it is likely the pitches will still be waterlogged as early in the year as April. Now part of the county of Avon, and once a port ranking second only to London, Bristol became a county in its own right in the 1373, prior to which the town centre north of the Avon was in Gloucestershire but the suburbs south of the river lay in Somerset.

It's possible to cross the Avon on the cycle-track on the east side of the M5 bridge but this is not recommended. The ridge walk from Clevedon past Cadbury Camp is very pleasant and an old railway line provides most of the route into Clevedon from Axbridge, but the access onto the cycle track at the south end of the M5 bridge is tortuous and through a housing estate (there is no direct access for pedestrians and cyclists from Gordano service station). At the north end there's a dreary 3m trudge along A403 past almost every kind of industry before there's access onto the Severn Way along the river to Aust..

One of Britain's most wonderful bridges, the Clifton Suspension Bridge (see front cover picture) was designed by Isambard Kingdom Brunel. The pylons were built in 1836-40, but due to financial difficulties the bridge itself was only completed in 1864, six years after Brunel's death. The iron chains were re-used from a bridge at Charing Cross which was taken down in 1861. There's a toll for vehicles to cross but there's no charge for pedestrians. After crossing over climb up to the left to where the observatory is and continue in the same direction for half a mile. Cross over an A-road onto Clifton Down. Pick up a path through an avenue of trees, but turn off left. Cross over the road junction at ST 566750, heading NW down Julian Rd. Fork left down Pitchj and Put Lane which leads to the tree-lined Mariners' Path past Stoke Bishop Church. A third of a mile further on turn right then left (a path cuts the corner off). Turn right at a T-junction but before long you'll be able to walk on a path between the road and a stream. At a road a slight detour to the east is necessary to join a new path in woodland by the stream. The valley is now steeper and the trees block out the houses up on either side.

The path crosses to the west side of the stream and remains on that side after crossing an A-road. After another third of a mile take the higher path to climb up to Henbury hillfort. From there take a path heading NE to Blaise Castle, a triangular folly with circular corner turrets which is open free of charge at weekends (see photo on page 4). It was built in 1766 by Thomas Farr. Continue past Blaise Castle House, built in 1796 for John Scandrett Harford, heading NE to the church at HENBURY, 4m from Clifton. Much of it dates from c1200 and the late 13th century and there is a good collection of monuments from 1695 onwards. From Henbury follow B4055 northwards for half a mile, passing a co-op. Amazingly this is the only shop encountered along the whole of this stretch of many miles into and out the west side of Bristol and you will not see any industrial premises at all. Turn left after the shop to get access onto the path which crosses the railway and heads north past stables. Turn left onto a track towards Berwick Lodge which crosses the M5. A path with a fine set of new metal kissing gates leaves on the right before the lodge and goes over Spaniorum Hill. Cross over two minor roads to reach the church at EASTER COMPTON, 7m from Clifton. The south doorway and chancel arch are Late Norman and the tower is 14th century.

Turn left down B4055 and pick up a path past the east side of the farms of Washingpool and Brynleaze. Go under the railway on a road and turn down the track which passes Rookery Farm, which is signed as a bridleway. Cross over a road just north of Torrs Farm and follow tracks through to a bend of a lane. Turn right and take the path on the left which goes over the M4 leading to the New Severn Bridge. Go past Holm Farm and off its approach road take the path northwards to Bilsham Farm. Cross over the road to another path which curves round to reach the village of AUST, 12m from Clifton and 260m from Land's End, where there's a pub and a good 15th century church with a tall west tower, and original roofs and font. There's a camp-site half a mile to the west at Old Passage. Just NW of Aust go under the M48 to obtain access onto the cycletrack which runs along the north side of the M48 for almost three miles as it crosses firstly the Severn estuary on the Old Severn Bridge built in 1961-6 and then the mouth of the River Wye, taking you from Avon over a short section of Gloucestershire at Beachley, and then into Monmouthshire (or Gwent) in South Wales.

From the intersection of the motorway and A466 there's access to a path leading round the south and east sides of the Bulwark estate which is named after the fort whose overgrown ramparts you'll pass after coming oit of shore-side woodland into the houses. Its almost another mile, partly path and partly road to the centre of the town of CHEPSTOW, 265m from Land's End. All services are available here. Isolated by a bend of the Wye on the east, and formerly known as Striguill, the town was closed off on the west in the 1270s by a wall with several D-shaped bastions. These defences remained fairly complete until the southern section was destroyed in 1918 to create a new shipyard, and two other breaches were made for roads in the 1960s and 70s, but the main street still runs through a square gatehouse mostly of the early 16th century. William Fitz-Osbern, Earl of Hereford, who died in 1071, founded the Benedictine priory near the bridge, the nave of which, with blocked Norman arches on each side, and a fine 18th century west tower, remains in use as the parish church. Fitz-Osbern also built the long rectangular keep forming the core of the splendid castle set on a ridge on the north side of the town with a sheer limestone cliff above the Wye (see photo on page 3). Now in the custody of Cadw (Welsh Heritage) it was the earliest castle in Britain to be built of stone, and an important bridgehead in the Norman invasion of South Wales. Between 1189 and 1245 the Marshal family, Earls of Pembroke, added two further courts at either end of the modest original baileys extending at each end of the keep, also providing several circular flanking towers (later cut down to mount cannon on their tops) and a main twin-towered gatehouse. Then in the late 13th century the Bigod earls of Norfolk built most of the apartments. They added at the SE corner a huge U-shaped tower rising from a rectangular base which is named after Henry Marten, kept prisoner in it by Charles II for his part in the trial and execution of Charles I in 1649. The castle required much repair after being wrecked during a siege by Parliamentary forces in 1648, when the wall west of Marten's Tower was breached by cannonfire. The carpark below the castle has a tourist information office and toilets and there's a museum across the road.

CHEPSTOW TO BEWDLEY

71m mostly ridge walking, starting on Offa's Dyke, part of Gloucestershire Way to cross the Forest of Dean, over May Hill, onto the Malverns, and then Worcestershire Way. Several steep climbs. Numerous sections of mixed woodland. Ever-changing views.

CHEPSTOW - ST BRIAVELS 9m all on Offa's Dyke Path except last mile on roads.

Aston Ingram

May Hill

Longhope

Micheldean

Abenhall

Drybrook

A4151

A4136

Sculpture Trail

B4226

Glos Way

B4234

Parkend

B4231

B4228
Castle

St Briavels

two miles

Hewelsfield

Offa's Dyke

Devil's Pulpit
B4228

Tintern

Lancaut   Tidenham

Wintour's Leap

St Arvans

CHEPSTOW

Cross the Wye on the bridge near the castle and take the path up on the right to join the Offa's Dyke coming in from its start at Sedbury Cliffs 1.6m to the SE. The trail is fairly well signed - just as well, since there's over 30 junctions of paths, tracks and roads in the next 7 miles. Cross over the road, and go past a tower. A mile from the bridge there's a short length on B 4228, then there's a fabulous half mile on top of cliffs above the Wye, including the spot known as Wintour's Leap. Go back on yourself right on B4228 (not too well signed here) to find a pair of loops of path east of the main road.There's a cut off path to the Gloucestershire Way at the end of the second loop, 2m from Chepstow. However, if you take this you'll miss the next section of the Offa' Dyke Path west of B4228, where you walk on the actual dyke itself, raised in 757 by Offa, King of Mercia, as a boundary against the Welsh. This section is heavily wooded but there's occasional glimpses of the Wye far below, and the extensive ruins of the Cistercian abbey of Tintern are visible from the rock outcrop known as the Devil's Pulpit. You could visit the abbey by taking the Wye Valley Walk out of Chepstow to keep on the west bank of the river, crossing the Wye at Brockweir to join the Offa's Dyke Path at SO 544015, after it crosses a steep valley with a clear length of the dyke on the southern side.

The path crosses a road, goes left a few yards at another road to pick up a track, off which leads a path up the hillside. After a third of a mile there's a short road section, then the path forks off right, climbing steeply between two hedges with trees. Keep on Offa's Dyke Path going left at a junction, but at SO 539030 leave the signed route to head right along a track round a double bend to turn right on a road to start a sequence of quiet roads to St Briavels. Follow the main road left when there's a fork in a third of a mile, pass a phonebox and a staggered crossroads, Turn left at a T-junction, and left again (despite St Briavels being signed straight on). Keep right on the upper road at a folk and this will bring you to to the castle and church of ST BRIAVELS. The church is a cruciform building with a Norman south aisle, a north transept and crossing of c1200. The tower over the crossing arches was removed c1830 and replaced by a porch-tower on the south side, whilst the chancel was rebuilt in 1861. Other parts are 13th century, as is the interesting tomb-slab inside. There is free access to the grounds of the castle, which is in the custody of English Heritage. It was a royal fortress serving as the administrative and judicial centre of the Forest of Dean. The early 13th century hall block and parts of the late 13th century twin-towered gatehouse with many portcullis grooves are still habitable and in use as a youth hostel. The dining room, now the scene of medieval banquets, occupies the lowest level of a chapel block projecting east. Originally there was a tower keep in the southern part of the courtyard. See p76. The village has a pub and there's B&Bs, but it has recently lost its shop and post office.

ST BRIAVELS - MAY HILL   16m via the Gloucestershire Way and other paths.

Take a path to the right off the road leading north past the west end of the church. Head over to the fence corner and keep left of it, hugging the contour. Pass through a gate and along the north side of a farm building, keeping north of the fence running east of it. The path drops down through woods and between paddocks, where taps have been provided for watering horses. Turn left round a bend on B4228 to reach the restricted byway on the right. Its tarmac for a short while, but eventually becomes just a rutted path out to Bream Cross, where you join the Gloucerstershire Way as it heads east along B4231 for a quarter of a mile until there's a path on the left. Cross over a track onto section of tarmac road and follow a path in the same direction when the road bends right. At Mill Hill, just over 3 miles from St Briavels, turn left then right on roads then take the pathb on the left. Cross a track, then turn right on a track and take a path on the right when it turns left. After half a mile go straight over at a five-way junction of paths and tracks. Turn right after the track bends left, cross over a road at SO 605080. Take the left fork opposite some houses. Turn left onto a track, but immediately turn right, heading north on a path through sessile oaks. Turn right at a track to cross over B4234 at the south end of Cannop Ponds and take the second left at a five-way junction, heading NE for quarter of a mile until turning northwards on a track. When the Gloucesatershire Way turns right at SO 612106 carry on straight ahead to turn right onto B4226. After a short distance the access to the car park, toilets and cafe at the start of the sculpture trail is on the left, 7.5m from St Briavels.

Visiting all 18 of the existing sculptures will take at least two and a half hours but you can see six of the most interesting ones on a fairly direct two mile route that will bring you back onto the Gloucestershire Way at SO 633145. From the cafe take the zig-zag path heading NE up to no 1, a gigantic wooden chair called Place. Cross over a track to head NE for a short distance, then turn left, heading north on shortcut A on the leaflet about the sculptures available at the cafe. At the bottom pass through a gate onto an old railway track. A short loop on the opposite side leads past no 4, the Black Dome, and no 5, Fire & Water Boats. Back on the railway track, heading NE, you soon come to No 6, Iron Road, a set of twenty wooden railway sleepers carved with images of fauna, flora and the forest's industrial past. These four sculptures all date back to when the trail was first established in 1986. More recent ones are no 7, Searcher, a wire deer just visible amongst vegetation on the right and side of the track, and no 8, In Situ, a mock industrial-archeological site on the short path between leaving the right side of the railway and the five-way junction where the Gloucestershire Way is rejoined.

The way recrosses the old railway and turns right on a path running east on the north beside of it. The path then turns north, crossing several tracks through Birch Wood. It feeds through to a road, off which you turn right on a path parallel to the south side of A 4136, which is eventually crossed in a mile, having crossed over A 4151 first, Cross a path on top of Harrow Hill, and when the path comes out at a crossroads at SO 659170, cross over, recross to the south side A4136 on a lane, and at the double bend take a path down a gully to cross over a road near a school. Cross a valley, turn left onto a road which bends right and then left. Take a road right off the second bend to the church of ABENHALL, 13m from St Briavels, The most interestiing features are the font and the tower, both 15th century, the latter set at the west end of a 14th century south aisle. Take the second of two paths left off the road past the church to go over Pool Hill and down to recross A4136 again just west of a pub. Take care on the heath opposite, as there isn't just one clear route. The way crosses a road and then turns rght down a track before turning left to come out at the church of LONGHOPE 15m from St Briavels, 24m from Chepstow. The west tower and nave are Norman, and the chancel and transepts are 13th century. Go north along the road by the church until the bend of A40, where there's a path almost opposite to a road, This road forms part of the Wysis Way, which offers an alternative route from the crossroads at SO 659170. This route involves more road-walking and is less rural but gives access to shops and places to stay in MICHELDEAN, where there's also a fine church with a 15th century outer north aisle wikth some old glass and several interesting monuments. After the confluence of the two ways turn right on a path to climb up from 165ft over a lane and onto the 985ft high summit of MAY HILL, offering fine views, and scene of May day frolics.

MAY HILL TO REDMARLEY D'ABITOT   10m, 7m on various paths, 3m on roads.

Great Malvern

Worcestershire
Beacon
A449

West
Malvern

B4232

Malvern
Hills

Little Malvern

Herefordshire
Beacon

Worcestershire

Obelisk

Eastnor
Castle

Herefordshire

Gloucestershire

M50

Bromsberrow

Redmarley
D"Abitot

A417

Pauntley

two miles

Newent
B4215

B4216

Aston
Ingram

May
Hill

From the top of May Hill take the path heading NNE to cross from Gloucestershire into Herefordshire for just the third of a mile downhill heading NE on another path to a corner of a road, where you turn right, back into Gloucestershire, down to the Yew Tree pub at Clifford's Mesne. Turn right past the pub, and find a path on the left just after a road on that side. Turn right at the cross-roads of hedged paths. Affer a short distance turn left on a track, then right at a crossroads, although you can take a shortcut through the field with pylons. The road bends twice and then there's a path on the left into the SW corner of Acorn Wood, Go left at a junction in the wood to reach the north corner. Then follow the path to the west of the field boundaries, heading NE to a track to a road which is crossed onto a path opposite, which goes through a community woodland and comes out on a road leading past toilets into Newent. There's more toilets on the car park in NEWENT, which is 29m from Chepstow, and there's several shops. A small town, noted for its Onion Fair held early in September, Newent has quite a number of old buildings and a museum in the Shambles. In a rebuilding of the 1670s at the church a wide new nave replaced a medieval nave and aisles which had collapsed, but a 14th century porch-tower with a spire remains on the south side. There are 13th century arches between the chancel and south chapel, and there are a number of interesting monuments, plus a Saxon cross-shaft in the porch. To the SW of Newent, east of Acorn Wood, is a birds-of-prey centre.

Follow the paths along the south side of a lake in public park north of the church, cross over B4215 on a path up to a crossroads of lanes. Take the lane heading NE to the T-junction at Littleford, where you cross over onto a path past a campsite and glasshouses. It then rises past orchards to Brand Green, 2m from Newent. Turn right on a road, then left onto a path across fields to PAUNTLEY. Take the track up to the farm west of the church. The sandstone church has fine Norman work in the chancel arch and south doorway, The south chapel is of c1430 and the west tower is 16th century. There are several interesting memorials inside. Dick Wihitting-ton, Lord Mayor of London c1400 came from the family that owned adjacent Pauntley Court, although the exist-ing building is 16th and 18th century. A path past the west side of it leads north to join a road heading north over Payford Bridge and up to a crossroads of roads and tracks. Turn right soon after crossing over and turn right at the end to reach a group of old timber-framed houses around the church of   REDMARLEY D'ABITOT, 6m Newent and 10m from May Hill. Theres a few mon-uments of interest, but the church was rebuilt in 1854 except for the tower, which is of 1738.

Beauchamp Fountain, north end of Malvern Hills (p36)

REDMARLEY D"ABITOT - WEST MALVERN 11m, all on paths, except 1m of road.

From Redmarley church head north on a road which bends to the NE and take a path on the left. Just past a house turn right on another path, keep south of another house and cross over A417 and then the Glynch Brook before turning left down the drive of Park Farm. Keep right onto a road which bends right. Take a left fork a quarter mile after crossing the M50. When the lane bends right take a path forking left and go right after a gate to get round a field and up to another road. Turn right, then left in a short distance, The path goes round the north side of a farm and heads NNW to join a road climbing up on the west flank of Chase End Hill, 13m from May Hill, the south end of an eight mile section of wonderful tracks heading north along the full length of the top of the Malvern Hills. As the road bends take the track on the right climbing the hill. At Whiteleaved Oak cross from Gloucestershire into Worcestershire by turning right on a road, then immediately left onto another path through woods with bluebells up to A438. Again there's a short right turn along the road before a track leaves on the left round the west side of Midsummer Hill. Go straight on at the crossing of tracks at the Gullet unless you want to make a detour westwards to read the inscriptions on the obelisk towering above Eastnor Park. It commemorates a son of the first Earl Somers, builder of Eastnor Castle 1m to the SW, which was begun in 1812 to a design by Sir Robert Smirke. Further east, south of the obelisk, is the moated platform of the medieval castle of Bronsil, a seat of the Beauchamp family. The last remaining polygonal tower collapsed into the moat a while ago.

From the Gullet the path heads NE through woods and then north over the bald tops of Swinyard Hill and Hangman's Hill, past a small cave and then up over the impressive outer ramparts of the huge Iron Age fort on the Herefordshire Beacon. On the highest point is a large Norman castle mound surrounded by a deep ditch. From here descend to the junction of A449 and B4232, where there's a carpark, toilets, a refreshments kiosk, and a pub called The British Camp. Walk along B4232 for a short way for access onto the path on the top of the ridge. After another two miles another road bisects the ridge at the Upper Wyche, where there's more toilets, and a pub (Wyche Inn) offering B&B just NE of the cutting. From the carpark on the west side a tarmac track leads to the 1400ft high summit of the Worcestershire Beacon (highest point south of Cross Fell beyond Appleby) 20m from May Hill, 45m from Chepstow Castle, and 310m from Land's End.

Head down northwards to a junction marked by a circular stone table with routes marked in various directions. One route is labelled to St Anne's Well, where there's a cafe and a chance to sample for free Malvern spring water, famous for containing nothing at all. Carry on past St Anne's Well if you want to vist GREAT MALVERN, a 19th century spa town where well-to-do people came to drink the waters and enjoy exercise and fresh air on the hills. It has a fair range of shops, and there's a tourist office and a small outdoor shop, although there's a better range of outdoor equipment at a shop a mile further down to the NE in Malvern Link. Malvern is a place that has several centres rather than one large centre, and altogether has a population of about 24,000 people, served by two stations. Great Malvern has a fine cruciform church of a former Benedictine priory. It contains Norman arcades with sturdy round columns, although most of the exterior and much of the furnishings, including painted tiles, choir stalls, and fine stained glass windows are 15th century. There's quite a collection of effigies and other features of interest. There's a small museum in the abbey gateway. A second but smaller and more mutilated Benedictine priory church remains in use 4m further south at Little Malvern.

You can pick up the start of the Worcestershire Way down by a fountain in Great Malvern, thus facing a steep climb, or if still on the ridge summit you can take a path heading NW over the crest of the hills from SO 767461 to 764465. At the latter point the way takes a very sharp bend back on itself and heads north for two thirds of a mile before dropping down onto the B4232 beside a pub called The Lamb, which also has a small foodstore. Going south from the sharp bend gives access to a spring of drinkable water above a school and the parish church of WEST MALVERN, dating from 1870. Further south there's a second pub, the Brewer's Arms, down a track from a carpark by the B4232. From the Lamb the Worcestershire Way then follows the road for 200yards before dropping down a long flight of steps to the left. Alternatively you can keep on the right-hand fork instead of forking left down to the pub. This path zig-zags down the hill within trees after coming to a viewpoint facing north. The snag is that you then have to cross B4232 diagonally to the left on a blind bend to reach the steps.

WEST MALVERN - BEWDLEY 25m via Worcs Way & Abberley cut-off. (3m roads.)

On the Malvern Hills the Worcestershire Way signs are low-level and inconspicuous. From now on there are new signposts clearly marking the way, which thus only requires a basic description. At the foot of the steps down from B4232 turn right onto Old Hollow, then left down a steep path, coming out on B4219 beside the Beauchamp Fountain (see p34), where you can obtain drinkable water, the last opportunity for this for many miles. The way then heads north along paths for a mile to cross A4103 near a pub. Paths then lead over Birchwood Common to Longley Green, where there's a short section along a road and a shop, 4m from West Malvern. . The next four mile section to where the River Teme is crossed on a footbridge to the Talbot Inn at KNIGHTWICK is mostly paths and tracks on a wooded ridge, but with the last half-mile along a road. The pub does accommodation and will allow backpackers to camp beside the river.

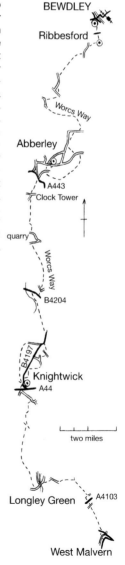

BEWDLEY

Ribbesford

Worcs Way

Abberley

A443
Clock Tower

quarry

Worcs Way

B4204

B4197
Knightwick
A44

two miles

Longley Green   A4103

West Malvern

The way follows B4197 for a short distance before making two awkward loops east of the road, rejoining it after 2m to pass another pub, the Admiral Rodney. A simpler and easier alternative is to use the track east of the river to Horsham Farm and then climb up on a lane. The amount walked on the B4197 works out about the same. Unless you want to visit the Norman church and shop at Martley carry along the way down west of B4197 to the east bank of the River Teme, followed by an awkward section, crossing a ploughed field to a farm and then heading eastwards back on itself for 200yards along B4204 to pick up a path climbing steeply up towards Hillend Farm. The climb is the start of a fine four mile section along a ridge with great views over the Teme valley. Its all path, except a short road section to get around Woodbury Quarry. At B4203 go left and immediately right to pass Abberley Hall, dating from 1846, now a school. You'll pass right beside the ornate clock tower of 1883 which is a landmark for miles around. Shortly after crossing A443 the way swings round to the right to use a 2m section of woodland ridgeway path along Abberley Hill, curving round a quarry at the east end. Although very pleasant this route adds an extra mile. A more direct route, rejoining the Worcestershire Way at Netherton Farm, is to use a mile of quiet lanes through Abberley village, where there's a pub (Manor Arms) and an old church, only ther east end of which, entered by a reset Norman doorway, is still roofed. If you need a shop you'll have to divert 200yards to the NW along A443 to SO 743674.

Just north of Netherton Farm the way takes a path heading NE across fields. Turn right onto the road, then left on a path which curves round left to Joan's Hole, where the Dick Brook is crossd by three small bridges. The way then climbs up on a ridge to Palmer's Farm, where there's a tap on the left hand side opposite the main house. After another short section on a road, turn right across a field (path is well marked) and then after crossing a stream, up through fields to Heightington. There's then two short road sections with a cut off path between them, before crossing the Little Lakes Golf Course. After another short road section a path brings you down into the churchyard at RIBBESFORD, which has a tap near the lych-gate. The church has two Norman doorways and the unusual feature of a 15th century arcade made of timber rather than stone. There was much rebuilding in 1877, after the church was struck by lightning. Go north from the church, cross under the A456 Bewdley bypass and paths then curve round right into the small but delightful Georgian river-side town of BEWDLEY, 336m from Land's End.

78m, almost 30m of it on canal towpaths, mostly rural and some sections very pretty. The rest mostly paths, with two fairly easy climbs over open heaths. Occasional mud or ploughed field, but mostly surprisingly easy to walk and navigate. Only 11m of roads.

BEWDLEY - KINVER   9m via route over top of Kinver Edge, using 3m of roads.

Bewdley offers all services and has a church of 1745 (tower of 1690) on an island in the middle of the main street. Stourport further downstream took the canal traffic and associated industries and Bewdley remained unspoiled. Originally the Worcestershire Way ran another 8m to Kingsford Country Park at the south end of Kinver Edge, following the west bank of the Severn for 3.5m to the footbridge at Upper Arley, where there's a pub and station. This is stiill usable but a shorter route is offered as follows. Follow A456 over Thomas Telford's bridge of 1795-8 at Bewdley, round two double bends and under the bridge carrying the steam trains of the Severn Valley railway. Turn off left beside Burns House and go right up Grey Green Lane. Turn left then immediately right up the lane to Lich Marsh Farm and then take the path NE across two fields to reach a lane beside a community woodland. Use the paths in the woods to reach the moated platform which is thought to have been the site of a fortress built in 1404-5 against the rebel Welsh led by Owain Glyndwr. Rejoin the road and turn right. After a while there is a path beside a road on top of a high sandstone cliff edge. Two thirds of a mile from the fort turn left onto a path between two hedges. Cross over a track onto another such path. It zigzags, becomes a track and comes out on A442 just over a mile NNW of Kidderminster parish Church. Go down the lane opposite, turn right at a T-junction, then left down a track. Go left onto B4190 for 350 yards and then right onto a path which leads to a track to the towpath of the Staffs & Worcs Canal. Use the towpath just as far as The Lock pub and go left on B4189 to reach either the track around Wolverley Church, a brick building of 1772 set on a cliff edge, or the lane below it. Stay on the lanes for two miles, turning right at SO 839829 to visit the 14th and 15th century church of KINVER containing a fine brass on a tomb,and then go east and north for 700yds to regain the canal towpath, 8m from Bewdley, A more scenic alternative, adding an extra mile along heathland tracks with fine views, is possible by turning off left on a track at SO 831813 and keeping left to reach the summit of Kinver Edge. This way you'll cross the Worcerstershire - Staffordshire county boundary on the edge, then reach a hillfort elevated at 550ft, and then drop down past the houses built into the sandstone cliffs at Holy Austin Rock. Turn right onto the road at the bottom to walk eastwards down the village street and thus pass a variety of shops, a pharmacy, and some toilets.

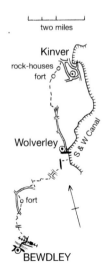

Rock-houses at Holy Austin Rock, north end of Kinver Edge

KINVER - PENKRIDGE   18m by canal & 5m mostly on roads

From Kinver follow the towpath of the Staffs & Worcs canal as it winds its way northwards. It goes under A458 and turns a corner to cross the Smestow Brook after 2m. After 6m SWINDON is reached, where there's a pub, and B4176 crosses over after another mile. There's suburbia for another mile, with several bridges, but also sandstone cliffs, and then three more miles of countryside up until the outskirts of Wolverhampton are reached at Castlecroft. However the houses are mostly screened off by hedges and trees, and the canal environment remains pleasant for three more miles passing under A454 and then A41 at Newbridge, where there's shops, a pharmacy, pubs and places to stay east of the canal. Pass a junction, 13m from Kinver, with another canal rising with 20 locks between here and the railway station 2m away in the centre of WOLVERHAMPTON, a city of 250,000 people offering all services. After another half mile join the towpath of the Shropshire Union canal leaving to the left. Another half mile brings you back in open country, and beyond the M54 there's a very pleasant cutting with wooden slopes above the canal and a fine bridge of 1826 by Thomas Telford carrying an avenue leading west for almost two miles to the Giffard family seat of Chillington Hall. Cross the canal on the track on the second bridge beyond, 18m from Kinver, and take a path immediately on the left to come out opposite the church of BREWOOD, a much rebuilt 13th century building with a later medieval west tower and spire, and four fine tombs of 16th and 17th century members of the Giffard family. There's shops, two pubs and a pharmacy but no signs of anywhere offering accommodation. The gothick folly house of c1750 called Speedwell Castle was built from the proceeds of betting on a racehorse called Speedwell belonging to the Duke of Bolton.

Take the road heading NE from the crossroads by the folly. Go over a crossroads after two thirds of a mile and take a path on the right when the road goes left. Cross the River Penk on a footbridge and come out on the A5 just east of where this road crosses the river. It lies on the line of the Roman Road of Watling Street and there was a Roman settlement a third of a mile further east. Walk in this direction until there's a lane (now not used by traffic) on the left. Go straight on at a junction and then left into Water Eaton Lane all the way to the embattled parish church of PENKRIDGE, a large 13th century building much altered in the 16th century and containing quite a number of monuments. There's a station nearby and in the village across the A449, 363m from Land's End, are shops, pubs and a pharmacy.

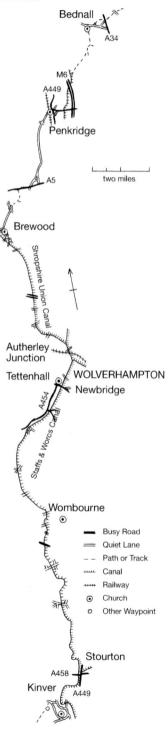

two miles

Busy Road
Quiet Lane
Path or Track
Canal
Railway
Church
Other Waypoint

PENKRIDGE - GREAT HAYWOOD   9m. 6m on varied paths. 3m on roads.

Speedwell Castle, a folly at Brewood

Essex Bridge over the River Trent

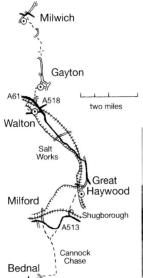

Head east down the main street of Penkridge for 300 yards to the Staffs and Worcs canal and join the towpath northwards for almost two miles, then head NE across fields on the Staffordsh Way from the second bridge after going under the M6. Cross a track, go through a belt of woodland and join a road heading north to the church at BEDNALL, a small building of 1846 with a tower of 1873. Turn right at the church and then left. At the fork keep right on what becomes a path over fields. Keep right at a junction of paths and bend left to cross over A34 and then another road. After crossing a third road you'll be at 650ft looking down east into Sherbrook Valley on Channock Chase. Continue north on the Staffordshire Way, following it round to the right at the five-way junction at SJ 579201 after a causeway section of track. After another half mile turn right onto A513 for half a mile. There's a proper path on the northern verge for the last part of this, before turning left into the Shugborough estate. You'll pass fairly close to the a folly called the Tower of Winds, and another, The Triumphal Arch, is visible on the hill behind to your left, before you pass the hall itself. Its a National Trust property (administered by Staffs County Council) with the usual gift shop, cafe and toilets in the stable block. Most of the hall is 18th century, the same period as the follies, but it has a core of 1693. It was the seat of the Queen's cousin, the photographer Lord Lichfield. The bridleway through the estate finally crosses the RiverTrent on the 16th century Essex Bridge, a narrow stucture with many cutwaters. Immediately afterwards there's access onto the towpath of the Trent and Mersey Canal heading north but if you need a post office or shop then head over the canal and under the railway bridge into the village of Great Haywood.

Shugborough Hall

GREAT HAYWOOD - CHEADLE 17m. 3m of towpath, 11m other paths, 3m of roads.

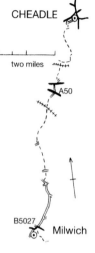

CHEADLE

two miles

A50

B5027

Milwich

Junction of canals just NW of Great Haywood

The Trent and Mersey canal towpath goes past salt marshes where there was once a saltworks (sign boards tell you about it). The church at WESTON has a fine 13th century tower. A pub and shop may also help make the short detour along A518 worthwhile. Leave the towpath on a track at the next bridge northwards and cross over the Trent Valley railway line on a high metal bridge. Cut diagonally across a field to cross over the dual carriagway A61 and go through fields east of the Gayton Brook to reach the church of GAYTON, 14m from Penkridge, a small building with a brick tower dated 1732 and a renewed Norman chancel arch. The defaced effigy and the arcades, one now blocked up, are also medieval.

Cross the Gayton Brook on a dead-end lane heading north to the east of the church and take a path over to a lane. Turn left and keep right at the fork, taking a path off right just as the road bends left half a mile after the fork. Go over the crossing of paths at SJ 981304 and follow the path as it bends NE down to cross a gully. Turn right onto a lane to cross a stream and then follow the path on its east bank into MILWICH, where there's a pub, although visiting the church with a medieval tower and a purple brick nave of 1792 involves a slight detour to recross the stream either by path or on B5027. Another pub at Coton to the SE is now closed.

From B5027 at Milwich take a lane in a wooded gully heading NE, passing Withysitch Farm. Take a path on the right after the crossroads by The Grove. Cross a stream and head down the track forming the western side of a triagular green at Morrilow Heath. Cross over at the NW corner and take a path bypassing to the right the house this lane leads to. Beyond the stream the old path is obscured but there's a new track to the corner of a tarmaced track. Head north on it for 300yards and the go through a gate on the rfight to pick up the line of an old track with hedges on either side towards Paynsley Hall, although in places you'll have to walk alongside it because its overgrown. The track improves past the hall (a farm) and goes over the River Blithe and the Trent Valley railway to pass Newton and go under the dual carriageway A50 and reach Totmonstow, 22m from Penkridge. Turn right, then left down a track, turning right on another track after crossing an overgrown disued railway line. After another half mile there's access onto the trackbed where a lane goes underneath it, and you can then use the railway as an access into the SW corner of the town of CHEADLE, which has a fair range of shops, and there's a campsite out at Hales Hall, a mansion of 1722 one mile to the NE. Cheadle is 389m from Land's End and has no medieval buildings, the anglican church dating only from 1837-9. Although not small it is outclassed by the amazing catholic church of 1841-6 with its lofty spire. Along with several adjoining buildings it was designed by A.W.Pugin.

CHEADLE - MACCLESFIELD   Easy 25m. 11m towpaths, 12m other paths, 2m roads

MACCLESFIELD

A537

A523

A54

two miles

Cheshire

Staffs

Rushton
Spencer

Rudyard
Lake

LEEK

A53

Cheddleton

Busy Road
Quiet Lane
Path or Track
Canal
Railway
Church
Other Waypoint

Kingsley

A52
A521

A521

A522

CHEADLE

Take A522 heading north out of the centre of Cheadle, and fork right on A521, passing a shop, and by
the Miners Rest pub after half a mile turn right down
a track leading to a path across fields. Turn left onto
a lane to pass Lockwood Hall, or right to visit the
restaurant at Thurnbury Hall. Cut a corner off to the
right just before the lane crosses the A521 at Kingsley
Holt. Pass a chapel and turn left to head NW along
the Staffordshire Way. After crossing A52 in half a
mile pass by the north side of the parish church of
KINGSLEY, mostly of 1820 and 1886, but with the
tower partly medieval. The way bends round and then
descends steeply beside a wildlife santuary, goes under a railway and over the River Churnet to meet the
towpath of the Caldon Canal heading NW along the
valley to the delightfully located Black Lion pub, just
over 5m from Cheadle, where the railway (a preserved
steam line) crosses the canal. At Cheddleton, 8m from
Cheadle, a bridge and level crossing give access to
the railway's headquarters and workshops. Beside
the canal is the Boat Inn, and after another half mile
the A520 crosses over and a short diversion south
down the main road gives access to a shop and the
parish church of CHEDDLETON with glass designed
by Ford Madox Brown and Burne-Jones and made
by William Morris in the 14th century chancel, where
the reredos is partly ancient and partly Morris's work.
The south aisle and west tower are 15th century and
the north arcade is 13th century.

A mile beyond the A520 bridge there's access off
to the right across the railway line and the river to a
bridge over a branch canal towards Leek. From its
towpath after a few yards heading west a path leads
up to the A53, which is followed westwards for 200
yards to take City Lane on the right. Immediately turn
right onto a path rising up through woods. It then follows the west side of the River Churnet for a mile and
meets the trackbed of an old railway line coming from
Leek, a mile and a half to the east, to run alongside
the east shore of Rudyard Lake. Follow it for four
miles, past a narrow guage railway and the end of
the lake and past the hill bearing the remarkable little late 17th century church of Rushton Spencer, with
evidence of older timber framing inside. Where the
trackbed passes over the River Dane it is blocked,
so take a path on the left 200yards further south, The
path crosses over, and rises beside, a tributary in a
wooded gully. After a mile turn right onto a lane, turn
right in nearly a mile. Instead of crossing the river
take a path across a field on the left. cross another
tributary marking the Staffordshire - Cheshire county
boundary and over the Macclesfield Canal to reach
its towpath. After six miles the canal passes within a
third of a mile east of the station and centre of MAC-
CLESFIELD, 414 miles from Land's End. A campsite
lies not far off the canal two miles south of the town.

MACCLESFIELD TO APPLEBY

123m. Three long sections of canal towpath totalling 49m.17m on mostly quiet roads. Three sections of moorland, two fairly short. Fairly easy navigation throughout.

MACCLESFIELD - DELPH 29m, almost all on canal towpaths.

Macclesfield is a town of 50,000 people offering all services and was once noted for its silk and cotton mills, many of which remain either empty or used for other purposes now. There was also a considerable trade in copper. The only relic of the town's medieval past is the parish church, mostly now a structure of 1898-1901, but with a medieval tower, a splendid south chapel with its own three storey west porch, and the best collection of monuments to be seen in any church in Cheshire.

The towpath of the Macclesfield canal can be used for 19m all the way to Portland basin, where there's a museum and toilets. The Middlewood Way running between Poynton and High Lane on an old railway trackbed can be used for a mile or two if you fancy a change. There's a flight of descending locks at Marple after the Peak Forest canal comes in from the SE, following a suburban section, and shortly afterwards the canal crosses the River Etherow and at the same place is itself crossed by a railway viaduct. Half a mile beyond there's no towpath through Romily Tunnel so you have to go over the top, beyond which there's a chapel at CHADKIRK, just south of the towpath. It has a south side of 1747 and a timber-framed medieval chancel. The remaining six miles to Portland Basin are mainly suburban, although there's a pleasant section south of Hyde where theres a wooded slope down to the River Tame on the west. For short sections either side of Flowery Field station at Hyde the towpath changes over to the east side. A good range of shops, pubs and a market lie within easy reach of where the A57 crosses the canal here at HYDE, once a major mill town.

From Portland Basin just south of Ashton-under-Lyme follow the recently restored Huddersfield canal for 8m to Dobcross. There's a supermarket just east of the basin, and a range of shops after 2m at newly tidied up STALYBRIDGE. There's a bar on the station platform. MOSSLEY, after 5m, offers a few more shops, and there's others at UPPERMILL. At Dobcross go a third of a mile west along A6052 and then take a path to New Delph along the east bank of the River Tame. Cross over A62 for a short path to a lane to Delph, 10m from Portland Basin.

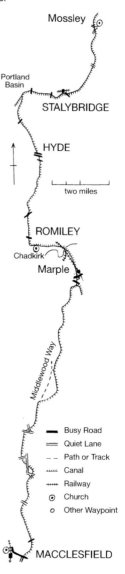

Mossley

Portland Basin

STALYBRIDGE

HYDE

two miles

ROMILEY

Chadkirk

Marple

Middlewood Way

━━ Busy Road
══ Quiet Lane
-- Path or Track
⊸⊸⊸ Canal
⊹⊹⊹ Railway
⊙ Church
o Other Waypoint

MACCLESFIELD

half mile

Chadkirk Chapel

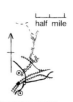

TODMORDEN

DELPH - NELSON   24m. 4m roads, 15m on paths, and 5m on canal towpath.

NELSON

two miles

Swinden Resr

Hurstwood resr

Cant Clough Resr

cross

A464

Stoodley
Pike

TODMORDEN
see opposite page

Pennine Way

Rochdale Canal

Blackstone
Edge Resr

M62

A672

Denshaw

A640

A6052

Delph   A62

A670

Dobcross

Uppermill

A669

Mossley

At Delph join A6052 for 100yards and then fork right and head
north on a track up from a fiveway junction to the pub at Heights.
Turn right on a lane and then left, going straight on along a path
when the initial track turns right. Descend by a ruined house to
a lane, turn right, and then at a T-junction go straight over on a
path which crosses the Tame to reach A640 just east of Denshaw,
where there's a pub and shop. Cross over and use paths to reach
where the Pennine Bridleway leaves the west side of A672 just
beyond a pub. This is a prettier and less exposed route than the
Pennine Way higher up a mile to the east, and passes the top end
of Piethorne Reservoir. After crossing a ridge elevated at 1150ft
there's a diversion westwards to a bridge over the M62, 5m from
Delph. A moorland track then leads to a lane at Lydgate. Go right
and then shortly left down a path to cross over A58. Descend to a
track, turn right, and after a third of a mile cross over the summit
level of the Rochdale Canal (see photo page 7) and head north
along its towpath over the border into West Yorkshire to the shops
and station at TODMORDEN, 12m from Delph. The youth hostel
of Mankinholes lies high up on a hillside 1.5m SE of the town.

Beyond Todmorden one option is to stay on the canal
for three more miles and then join the Pennine Way for
23m to East Marton as it goes over Heptonstall Moor, past
the Walshaw and Ponden reservoirs, and through Cowling
and Lothersdale. This route has great views but is boggy
and exposed in parts, only passes one small shop, and
means an extra 2700ft of steep climbing. The signing to
keep you on the way is less than adequate in several places, although its worse if youy are travelling southwards
on it. There's a hut sheltar with drinkabloe water nearby
at Top Withins (SD 981454).If blessed with good weather
you could have gone up to the Pennine Way earlier, at Lit-
tleborough, to enjoy the views from the monument of 1858
at Stoodley Pike. Much of the way here is on flagstones.

From a lower and easier route than the Pennine Way join A464
in Todmorden until beyond the market. Turn right up Wellington Rd
and go up Stansfield Rd to find a bridge over a railway. Go right
then left ujp The Hollins and through to turn right up Hole Bottom
Rd. Take a path left to cross a stream on a bridge. It rises to meet
a bridleway hugging the 340m contour NW for two miles. At SD
914274 (not long after passing a cross on the right in a field) go
uphill on a road, then left to pass Bank Top Farm. Drop down to
a small bridge andturn right to pass another farm before climbing
up to walk NW on the Long Causeway road for half a mile. Turn off
right on the Burnley Way. The track leads to a path (not on maps)
following a big pipe to the Cant Clough Reservoir, where you walk
over the dam and cross over a track before going left, After passing the east side of Hurstwood Reservoir go left for a few yards,
then right up the steep bank to join a lane heasding west. Turn right
and then left at the SW corner of Swinden Reservoir to join a road.
Go right, then left on a track opposite a pub. At a cross of roads
and tracks take the road hea`ding north for a mile to the cross at
Haggate. Turn left, then right on a path over a golf course. From the
crossroads at 856364 head north but keep left and turn left down
Lomeshaye Rd to fine a garage shop at the bottom. Cross over
A56 and go left at the bottom to cross over the Leeds and Liverpool canal and join its towpath just half a mile west of Nelson.

NELSON - SETTLE   24m. 12m of canal towpath, 6m on other paths, 6m on roads.

NELSON lies 467 from Land's End and has a fair range of shops, with a big supermarket by the canal not long after you join it. It was named after a pub dating from the area of the naval hero and the first cotton mill opened in 1780. This section of the Leeds and Liverpool canal was opened in 1801 and weaves quite a lot as it follows the contours.

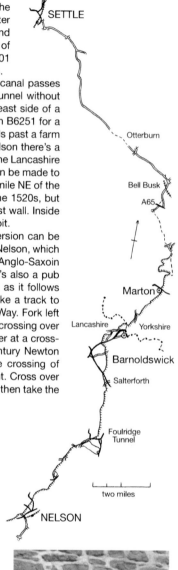

After two miles there's a series of locks as the canal passes a small reservoir and then there's a mile long tunnel without a towpath. Cross over a road to a path on the east side of a small reservoir, Cross a track, and eventually join B6251 for a short distance heading east until a track left leads past a farm onto a path back to the canal. After 6m fromNelson there's a pub at Salterforth. Two miles further, just before the Lancashire - Yorkshire county boundary a short diversion can be made to visit the church of BARNOLDSWICK, isolated a mile NE of the village. The south aisle and west tower are of the 1520s, but there's a triplet of 13th century lancets in the east wall. Inside are Jacobean box-pews and a three-decker pulpit.

After another two miles another short diversion can be made to visit the church of MARTON, 11m from Nelson, which has a Norman tower and a fine fragment of an Anglo-Saxoin cross carved with figures and interlacing. There's also a pub here. After another half mile ignore the towpath as it follows the canal round a series of sharp bends and take a track to the right which is also the northbound Pennine Way. Fork left off it after 300yards and briefly regain the canal, crossing over it, and then leaving it finally by going straight over at a cross-roads. Follow a good track down past 17th century Newton Hall and Ingber House and stay on it until the crossing of tracks below pot Haw Farm, where you turn right. Cross over A65 onto a path leading to the road to Bell Busk, then take the lane to OTTERBURN, 17m from Nelson

Go up a track through the Crook Beck Plantation, now owned by the Woodland Trust and onto a path over Hellifield Moor. This leads to a dead-end road leading past a second woodland in the care of the trust, and then past the waterfall of Scaleber Force. Finally there's a steep descent down into SETTLE, which has a junction station and a good range of shops and places to eat and stay. The church dates only from 1837 but there's a house dated 1679 called The Folly in the High St, and the Shambles in the Market Square is of about the same period.

Stainforth Force waterfalls, River Ribble, near Settle

Norman window in Marton Church

SETTLE - HAWES   20m. 4m of riverside paths, 2m of roads, 14m of Pennine Way.

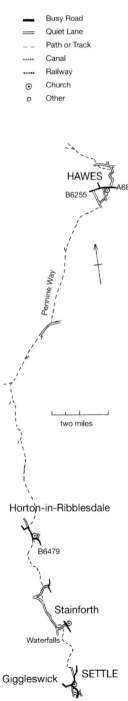

— Busy Road
= Quiet Lane
_ _ Path or Track
⏆⏆⏆ Canal
⊹⊹⊹ Railway
⊙ Church
o Other

HAWES
B6255   A684

Pennine Way

two miles

Horton-in-Ribblesdale

B6479

Stainforth

Waterfalls

Giggleswick   SETTLE

The Folly at Settle

Take the B6479 out of Settle but when the main road goes under the railway go left up to the campsite at Langcliffe Place. There's a path between it and the river. Cross the River Ribble half a mile after crossing a lane to find a path on the west bank up to the waterfalls at Stainforth Force, 2m from Settle, where there's another campsite. Go west on a lane for 300yards and then turn right on another lane. After just over a mile use the cut-off path down to another lane. Go past a quarry pool and then turn left on a track just before a bridge over the river. The track leads to a river bank path. Cross over the river on a footbridge a mile after the track went under the railway. Another path then brings you into HORTON-IN-RIBBLESDALE, 6m from Settle, which offers places to stay, a station, a pub and a shop. The church appears mostly late medieval externally but the south doorway, the font, and the western parts of both arcades are all Norman work of the 12th century.

Follow B6479 for a third of a mile to a crossroads and then follow the Pennine Way up a track on the right. Either stay on the way and turn left with it after three miles, or take another path forking left in a mile to run below a series of crags. Its a short cut, although care is needed to stay on the correct path. You'll climb up to rejoin the Pennine Way at Calf Holes. After two more miles go right on the track serving as both Dales way and Pennine Way. Looking back from here there's views of the Ribblehead Viaduct carrying the Settle and Carlisle Railway. After a mile and a half there's a mile section of unfenced road before the Pennine Way leaves to the left to go along the west flank of Dodd Fell. After two and half miles it forks to the right and descends to a lane. Cross over and follow this well signed section of the vway through Gayle and then along the NW bank of the Duerley Beck to reach the centre of HAWES, a nice little town with narrow streets, and a fair range of shops, although the church is only of 1851.

HAWES - KIRKBY STEPHEN   15m, mostly mountain paths. Barely 2m of roads.

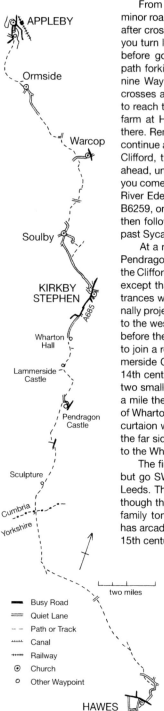

APPLEBY

Ormside

Warcop

Soulby

KIRKBY
STEPHEN

A685

Wharton
Hall

Lammerside
Castle

Pendragon
Castle

Sculpture

Cumbria

Yorkshire

two miles

━━ Busy Road
═══ Quiet Lane
- - Path or Track
⌒⌒⌒ Canal
+++++ Railway
⊙ Church
o Other Waypoint

HAWES

From the centre of Hawes follow the Pennine Way on a minor road heading NNE and then NW on a path immediately after crossing the River Ure. There's a pub at Hardraw where you turn left onto a road just long enough to cross a stream before going right on a path. After another mile take the path forking off left which hugs the contour whilst the Pennine Way continues climbing. The path passes two barns, crosses a road after two miles and climbs through conifers to reach the top of Tarn Hill at 530m. Descend to the ruined farm at High Dyke and turn right at the crossing of paths there. Remaining betweeen the 400 and 450m contours you continue along an old drove road named after the Lady Anne Clifford, two of whose castles, Pendragon and Appleby lie ahead, until after three miles from the farm, 9m from Hawes, you come to a sculpture, first of series along the valley of the River Eden, into which you'll now descend. Turn right along B6259, only to turn left after a few yards, cross the river, and then follow the sequence of footpaths along the west bank past Sycamore Tree Farm and Shoregill.

At a road recross the river on a road to visit the ruins of Pendragon Castle set on a ditched mound. Probably built by the Cliffords in early 14th century, it looks like a Norman keep, except that buildings that early never have ground level entrances with portcullis grooves as we have here. The diagonally projecting stair turret is an addition of the 1360s. Return to the west bank of the river, following the road for 250yards before there's a track on the right. When the track bends left to join a road take a path on the right past the ruins of Lammerside Castle. A timber framed hall probably adjoined this 14th century structure containing a fine upper chamber and two smaller rooms over a series of vaulted cellars. After half a mile the path joins a track which leads past the west side of Wharton Hall. The north range and the gatehouse and high curtaion wall facing towards you are all 16th century, but on the far side is a 15th century hall and chambers. It belonged to the Wharton family, who also held Lammerside.

The final mile into KIRKBY STEPHEN, is NE along A685, but go SW along this road if you need a train to Carlisle or Leeds. There's a fair range of shops and places to stay, although the youth hostel has now closed. There's a Wharton family tomb and other old memorials in the church, which has arcades and a north transept of the 13th century, a wide 15th century south aisle, and a 16th century west tower.

Eden Valley Sculpture

KIRKBY STEPHEN - APPLEBY   11m. 3m of roads, rest mostly paths near river.

Almost opposite Kirkby Stephen church turn left, then immediately right and keep left. This brings you out on a two mile lane to SOULBY, although as a slightly longer alternative to the second mile you can turn right onto a path on an old railway embankment for half a mile, then drop down left to a track. Go right at the crossing of tracks, then left on a lane into the village. There's no shop, but at least one house offers B&B and there's a small single-chamber church dating from 1662. Take the road north out of the village and when it turns left carry on northwards on a path past Sikeside. Cross over a road onto another path to the farm lane beyond Ploughlands. Take another path on the right to stay beside the river until the road bridge that gives access to WARCOP, a slight diversion, where the church has 13th century transepts and a 15th century south aisle and west front added to a Norman nave. A castle once lay to the east, and there is a 16th century hall. To pick up the next path along the SW side of the river go a short way in the other direction from the bridge and village. Keep left when the paths fork, climbing up slightly. At the bridge at Blacksyke still remain south of the river, initially on a track until there's a path on the right which climbs behind a strip of trees above the river. It eventually becomes a track, and then a road into ORMSIDE. The hall is partly the work of the Hilton family in the 17th and 18th centuries, but it contains a 14th century tower built by the Bartons. Set upon a mound opposite is a Norman church with a 16th century chancel, quite an interesting building. Don't be tempted by the bridleway leading north past the church since there's no bridge over the river. Instead go west at the crossing of tracks south of the church to use the path, partly in woodland, following the west bank of the Eden for the final two miles into Appleby, which is 537 miles from Land's End.

APPLEBY offers all services and has a station with trains to Carlisle and Leeds. Once the county town of Westmorland, the town has two medieval churches, although only St Lawrence's church remains in use. It is a typical long, aisled and embattled north country church, mostly of the 14th and 15th centuries, although the lower parts of the tower are Norman and the north chapel is 17th century. Inside is a fine organ case of c1540. At the other end of the town's wide main street (which has a Moot Hall of the 1590s lying iaolated on one side) lies the castle, a possession of the Clifford family from 1269 until the death in 1676 of the Countess Anne Clifford, whose tomb lies in St Lawrence's church. It then passed to the earls of Thanet. Partly 14th century and partly 17th century, the apartments at the east end are still habitable. The square tower keep at the west end (also still roofed) and parts of the curtain walls date back to the time of Hugh de Morville c1170.

Norman tympanum in Orton Church

Orton Hall   *Lammerside Castle*

APPLEBY TO NEWCASTLETON

59m. Section of Pennine Way to Alston, railway line to Hadrian's Wall Path, then mostly quiet lanes over the Border to Newcastleton apart from two short moorland paths.

APPLEBY - ALSTON 23m, mostly on Pennine Way, with one long climb. Just 3m on roads.

From Appleby follow B6542 over a bridge over the River Eden, and after half a mile take the right fork leaving under the A66 dual carrageway. Take the bridleway signed Powis House off the main road feeder loop. Turn right at the crossroads of paths at NY 673222. The path passes left of a house and then drops down to a bridge over the railway. Turn right onto a track, and then left for 100yds along a road to find another path on the right, leading through a farmyard. Cross over a road and follow field boundary down to where the there is a junction of paths and a picnic table near a footbridge. Shortly after crossing turn right onto a track. At junction of paths at the approach to DUFTON, go straight on (not shown on map) down to a footbridge, and then up into the village, which is arranged around a green. There's a youth hostel, a pub, and a shop-cum-post office & cafe, although its only open for a couple of hours in the morning and again later in the afternoon.

Go past the pub and take the track heading north, which is the Pennine Way. Over 4 miles it climbs 2100 feet onto Knock Old Man. An easier way to make the climb is to take the faint path heading north after the new footbridge over the Swindale Beck (NY 700785). This follows a wall more or less hugging the 420m contour and leads to the tarmac service road to the aircraft control centre on the top of Great Dun Fell, where you rejoin the Pennine Way. Another two miles, much of it on recently laid paving slabs, brings you over Little Dun Fell, where there's a rudimentary windbreak, and onto the top of Cross Fell, where there's a cross-shaped wind-break near the trig point. Half a mile of path, not always well defined, brings you down onto a track leading east and then NE, which served the former mines here. One mine building remains in use as an open bothy or mountain hut known as Greg's Hut, beyond which the condition of the track improves. The track eventually becomes a tarmac road running down into GARRIGILL, which has a shop and pub. The village hall toilets are accessible from both outside and inside. Indoor camping may be allowed in the hall, and there's space for a couple of tents behind it. In the form of paths across riverside fields which require many stiles the Pennine Way continues for 4 miles to ALSTON, a small former mining town with pubs, a chemists, hospital, and several shops, including an outdoor equipment shop, and a healthfood shop. The youth hostel is now closed. Toilets and a cafe are available down at the terminal station of the narrow guage railway built in 1983-99 to replace the original standard guage branch railway from Haltwhistle opened in 1851-2 and closed in 1976.

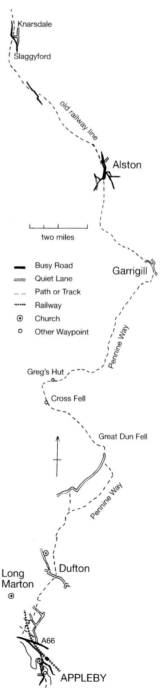

Knarsdale

Slaggyford

old railway line

Alston

two miles

Garrigill

— Busy Road
= Quiet Lane
- - Path or Track
++++ Railway
⊙ Church
○ Other Waypoint

Pennine Way

Greg's Hut

Cross Fell

Great Dun Fell

Pennine Way

Dufton

Long Marton

A66

APPLEBY

ALSTON - GILSLAND Easy 16m, half of it on old ailway trackbed. 2m on roads

From Alston station follow the path along the old railway trackbed for 8 miles as far as the 30m high LAMBLEY VIADUCT, from which there are fine views. The path is narrow for the first 3m to Kirkhaugh whilst it flanks the narrow guage railway, but is wider further north, and it provides a more direct and level path than the nearby section of the Pennine Way with all its stiles and gates. However, there's a very awkward diversion around the former Lambley station which is a private residence. This entails dropping down to the level of the River South Tyne. Follow the signs back up many steps onto the viaduct to cross it, read the notice board about it, and turn off left just before the site of Coanwood station. Alternatively you can cross the river on the footbridge just north of the viaduct. Either route brings you down onto a path across the meadows east of the river. Water can be collected from a tap in the churchyard at Lambley, which is a short diversion off the viaduct access steps. The church itself is of 1885. The only other service available along this section (most of which lies within Northumberland) is a B&B in Slaggyford. After crossing over a new road the path goes through the grounds of FEATHERSTONE CASTLE which belonged to the Featherstonehaughs until 1779. Much of this impressive building dates from 1812-20 but it incorporates a 14th century L-plan tower house at the SW corner, and the west range facing you may be partly 13th century. Before coming opposite the castle the path passes through the remains of a prisoner-of-war camp used to house German officers in the period 1945-8, lying 10m from Alston.

Just beyond the castle turn left onto a road for a few yards and then cross the river on a footbridge to use the path on the west bank. Turn left onto a road which curves round to the right whilst climbing. Just before meeting A69 after 2miles there's a drive on the left to BLENKINSOPP CASTLE, a ruined and much modified and extended 14th century residence of the Blenkinsopp family. It became the offices of a colliery in the late 19th century. A pub and restaurant lie in an adjacent building. Cross over A69 onto a path leading through meadows east of the Tipalt Burn. You can cut a little corner off by following the burn bank after crossing it. When the burn swings west you go through a gate, keeping a wire fence immediately to the right. A stile then leads onto a path behind a house and through to B6318 at GREENHEAD, 13m from Alston. There's a pub and tearoom on either side of the main road to the west of the bridge over the burn. Go a few yards eastwards up the B-road to find a path through a farmyard. This leads through to THIRWALL CASTLE, below which there's a tea-room and B&B and you join Hadrian's Wall Path, going westwards. There's free access to the ruined 14th century castle, an L-plan building built by the Thirwall family using small squared stones taken from Hadrian's Wall, set on a bluff above the Tipalt Burn. It was captured and wrecked by the Scots in the 1640s. The wing contained private rooms opening off two upper levels of large but rather poorly lighted public rooms set over a cellar in the main block.

From the castle a path heads SW to cross the railway and reach B6318. Where the path leaves the left-hand side of the road after 150yards there's a short section of the lower part of HADRIAN'S WALL. Between here and GILSLAND, 2m to the west,   and 39m from Appleby, where there's two pubs near the line of the well-signed path, and a shop a bit further away in the village centre, there's only buried footings of the wall itself. However the ditch on the north side of the wall mostly still remains in good condition. The wall was named after the Emperor Hadrian, who in AD122 visited Northern England and ordered the construction of this 72 mile (80 Roman miles) barrier between Bowness on Solway and Wallsend. Originally the western section of the wall was built of turf and only later replaced in stone. Opposition to the frontier from the northern tribes proved fiercer than expected, necessitating moving the supporting troops up from forts further south into new forts built astride the line of the wall itself, as at Birdoswald (see page 50). The military road to the south was built somewhat before the wall itself. South of it lay a ditch flanked by ditches forming a southern boundary known as the Vallum to the military-only zone. Not long after completion the wall was abandoned for a generation and a new frontier established further north. By the early 3rd century, however it had been restored as the permanent frontier, although it was damaged during revolts of 296 and 397, and finally abandoned by the early 5th century. The remains of the wall and its forts are now a World Heritage Site in the custody of English Heritage.

Milecastle 48 on Hadrian's Wall

GILSLAND - BEWCASTLE   8m. Varied paths for 6m, 2m on quiet roads.

Awkwardly perched on ground sloping down from south to north above the west bank of the Poltross Burn at Gilsland are the ruins of MILECASTLE 48 (in Cumbria), a small enclosure with north and south gateways containing two barrack blocks. About half of the next mile of wall still remains, together with both of the turrets which divided it into three sections, this being the usual arrangement along the wall. The turrets were built before the wall itself, and on either side of them are short stubs of wall 3m thick, which was the original intended width. There's also remains of the east abutment of a bridge carrying the wall over the River Irthing, which now lies further west and is crossed by a brand new footbridge. After it there's a 150ft climb to the remains of MILECAS-TLE 49, which is similar in plan to the other one. The next turret further west was later replaced by BIRDOSWALD FORT. As with the other forts an entrance fee is payable (access to the wall itself is free). There's a cafe, toilets and hostel here, beyond which there are no services of any kind until Newcastleton. Within the fort lie remains of a medieval tower house and of a defensible farmhouse or bastle of c1600.

Opposite the fort entrance is an indistinct bridleway leading over to B6318, which is followed westwards for 300yards until there's another bridleway leading NW. This one isn't signed, but it is distinct, and fenced on both sides. From here there are clear views of the 9m high remaining fragment of Triermain Castle at a farm half a mile away to the SW. Built c1340 by the Vaux family, it passed to the Salkelds, and then the Dacres. Turn right when you reach a track, and go through a gate on the left after 200 yards. Go over a small stile and cross the neck of the promontory projecting north above King Water. There's no sign of the holy well marked on the map. The indistinct path descends through woodland to a bridge and then climbs up to Palmer Hill Farm. The right of way follows the farm track westwards to a road leading northwards for just over a mile to Spadeadam Farm. The bridleway leading NNW from here is a bit tricky to follow. The faint tracks on the ground head north, but the actual route goes further west. Keep SW of the new woodland, find the rock outcrop at 578716, and then climb further until the gateway at 576718 is visible. A faint track then leads to another gate at 575719. From here there's a good view westwards, making the effort and navigational difficulties worthwhile. Stay east of the wall beyond here and from 570727 there's a good enough path to follow down to a track beside a farm. After a few yards on the track turn right on a road to BEWCASTLE, 49m from Appleby. There's no services here and only a few houses but there's a good selection of ancient monuments. Earthworks remain of a hexagonal Roman fort (an outpost of Hadrian's Wall) in the northern section of which lies the ruins of a 13th century castle of the Swinburne family which later passed to the Middletons. It had ranges of apartments on either side of a small court and a square gatehouse facing west. The church has a 13th century east end with triple lancet windows and an 18th century tower. Beside it lies the finely carved shaft of a Saxon cross with a runic inscription commemorating King Alcfrith, who lived in the late 7th century. This cross and a similar one at Ruthwell in Dumfriesshire are the finest relics of their period in the whole of Britain. On the south side of the churchyard is a building containing an exhibition about the history and fauna and flora of this remote Cumbrian parish.

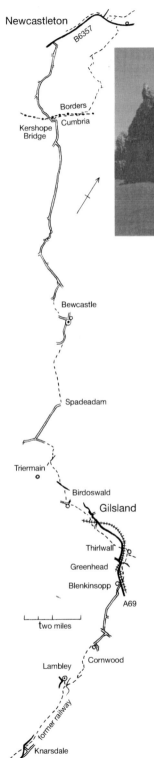

Bewcastle: castle ruins

Bewcastle cross

BEWCASTLE - NEWCASTLETON 12m mostly roads

From Bewcastle take the unfenced road westwards for 350 yards until a footpath is signed on the right. This leads past the northern ends of two small woods, over a bridge and onto a bend of an unfenced road heading north. After half a mile the road bends east and a short-cut path is signed through the field down to a gate just east of where the road fords the Bothrigg Burn. There's a bridge for pedestrians, and another at a second ford another 400 yards further on. The road then climbs to a hilltop junction. Keep right for Blackpool Gate, and go left 200yards past the chapel after the bridge. After 3m turn right beside a former pub and after a mile there's Kershope bridge, on the border with Scotland, 592m from Land's End, 55m from Appleby. You enter what used to be the southern end of Roxburghshire, part of the Scottish Middle March in the days of the Border Reivers, now part of Borders Region. Its then another 4m by road to the square at NEWCASTLETON, where there are two pubs, a food shop, a pharmacy, and a hardware shop. There are toilets in a lane leading NW off the square and there's occasional bus services to Carlisle. If you don't require these services its possible to bypass Newcastleton, on an alternative route which doesn't save any distance but reduces the amount of roadwalking by nearly three miles. Turn right at Kershope Bridge, and cross the river into Scotland on a track a mile further east. After a third of a mile take the left track climbing uphill. Keep right at NY 514860, turn left at 515863. Keep right after crossing a stream, but turn left at 507866. This will lead through to Dykecrofts, where there's an office, exhibition centre and toilets. Turn right and then take the path forking left over Priest's Hill, which is now part of a trail. This leads through to B6357. Turn left to cross Liddel Water and then turn right on a track up through two gates to reach the railway trackbed.

NEWCASTLETON TO WEST LINTON

64m. Old railway line, then mixture of mostly quiet roads and short sections on mountain paths, some of which require good map reading skills, preferably with a GPS as well.

NEWCASTLETON - HAWICK   Easy 20m mostly along trackbed of old railway line.

At the north end of Newcastleton its possible to get onto the unoffical footpath along the trackbed of the former mainline railway from Carlisle to Edinburgh. The railway offers easy level walking with fine views. Short diversions off it are necessary occasionally but on the whole its surprisingly devoid of obstructions. The viaduct over the Hermitage Water was removed about thirty years ago so its necessary to descend from the embankment down to a track back to B6357 to cross the river. About 150 yards after the bridge, just before buildings on the right, a track on the left through trees leads back towards the railway. Alternatively follow B6357 for 300yards and then use the farm track mentioned in the previous paragraph. Having regained the trackbed look to the right to see the earthworks of OLD CASTLETON, seat of the barony of Liddel held by the de Soulis family in the 13th century The inner enclosure has steep drops to the Liddel Water and a tributary and the outer enclosure has a high rampart and deep ditch. Not far beyond is a shed built over the trackbed but the gates at each end open easily and there wasn't any problem with walking through. Further on two short sections beside where cows trample the trackbed are fenced off to provide walkers with a clearer pathway through.

At Steele Road follow a track leading off east to a lane. Turn left and rejoin the railway by clambering up the embankment at the side of a bridge over another lane which leads through to B6399 not far south of where a lane leads west from it for a mile to the impressive ruin of HERMITAGE CASTLE. The diversion to visit the castle and then follow B6399 north for 3 miles to Whitrope Siding adds one mile overall and increases the amount of road-walking by six miles. In the care of Historic Scotland (entrance fee payable), the castle has a main block with four corner towers or wings and dates mostly from the 14th and 15th centuries. Here in 1566 the wounded Earl of Bothwell was visited by Queen Mary, who rode over from Jedburgh and back in a day, earning herself a fever.

Not far beyond Steele Road the trackbed now has offiicial status as a footpath and cycleway, being joined from the right by a track from the lane. Three miles from Steele Road is Riccarton Junction, where a branch line went off to Kielder. A short length of track has been relaid by the platform here, and two miles further on at the site of Whitrope Siding a heritage centre is being set up and there's another length of track leading towards Whitrope Tunnel. The society here hopes eventually to run trains from Hawick to the junction and then on to both Kielder and Steele Road. The restored railway will be single track on a trackbed originally filled by a double track main line so there will be room for the cycletrack to remain alongside. Ignore any signs about not proceeding any further. They only apply to vehicles, and walkers should always be able to get through although there may be temporary diversions whilst track is actiually being laid and cranes, etc, are present. The tunnel is not open to walkers but a new bridleway has been created for a mile over the top. The 160ft climb is enough to obtain good views northwards.

The cycleway leaves the railway at Shankend, but walkers can still go over the viaduct, although officially they too are supposed to slip down to the right, go under the viaduct, and turn right twice along a sequence of tracks to rejoin the railway trackbed. Just beyond where the mansion of Stobs Castle is visible on the right the trackbed is blocked by trees and a stile on the left leads into a field. Cross two more fields before reaching a road leading down under a viaduct. Under the viaduct look left to see a gate into a field. After 250yards its possible to regain the trackbed, although there's another short diversion soon after because a bridge has gone. Beyond Flex there's further blockages so turn left onto the lane and then turn right at the footpath sign. Turn left at a gate after a climb, cross a field, and through another gate onto a path which leads to a lane into the south end of HAWICK, 79m from Appleby. With a population of about 14,000 this is the largest town in Borders region and offers a good range of shops and other services. You'll pass the motte of the Lovells' earth and timber castle on the way in, plus some toilets with taps and sinks, and beside the bridge over the river is a much altered 16th century tower of the Douglases of Drumlanrig, recently restored to form part of a tourist information centre. A monument at the NE end of the High St commemorates a victory by the local men over an English force in 1514 at a time when the Scots' spirits were low after the defeat and death of James IV at Flodden the previous year.

HAWICK

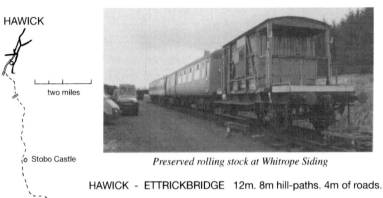

Preserved rolling stock at Whitrope Siding

two miles

Stobo Castle

former railway

Whitrope

Hermitage Castle

Riccarton Junction

B6399

Steel Road

former railway

Old Castleton

B6357

Newcastleton

HAWICK - ETTRICKBRIDGE 12m. 8m hill-paths. 4m of roads.

Cross the River Teviot in the middle of Hawick, almost opposite where you arrived in town. Take the path westwards along the north bank of the river. In the park follow the signs for the walled garden. Staying on the river bank is a slightly longer way round. After joining a road turn right then left up to Brieryhill, where accomodation is available. Beyond the farm the road becomes a track. The turn off to the left half a mile beyond the farm isn't that obvious although there is a sign. Turn right along B711 for two thirds of a mile and then turn right up the lane climbing steeply below the old mansion of HARDEN, home of the Scott family, with the oldest parts dated 1671 and 1691. It replaced an older tower which James VI had destroyed in 1592, the then laird and his father "Auld Wat" being amongst the most notorious Border reivers.

After three miles from B711 turn left on a track which winds down to a bridge over Ale Water, once the boundary between the counties of Roxburgh and Selkirk. As the track climbs leave it to follow a wall, going through a narrow gate and crossing two fields down to a bridge over Todrig Burn. Turn left and then fork right on a track past the north side of TODRIG, 8m from Hawick, which is a much-altered old tower of the Scotts of Whitslaid (a farm 1m to the south). Either follow the track to Langhope and take the path up through the farmyard or take the cut-off path east of the burn, which is signed. Both paths are clear until they converge. The path shown on the map from there is indistinct, so follow paths that are visible firstly westwards, and then NW to the middle of the south side of Alemoor Loch. Follow the shore of the loch, crossing a burn on stepping stones and going over a stile to find a good path going NW from the NE end of the loch, round the west side of Helmburn Hill to ETTRICKBRIDGE. Steps to the left cut off a corner down to where B7009 crosses Ettrick Water, just over 32m from Newcastleton.

Tower at Hawick

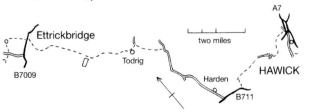

Ettrickbridge

Todrig

B7009

two miles

Harden

A7

HAWICK

B711

ETTRICKBRIDGE - PEEBLES   18m, mostly over moorland paths. 2m of roads.

After crossing Ettrick Water turn right past the church on a track leading out beside a cemetery. Follow the field boundary and cross Tower Burn below KIRKHOPE TOWER, a mid 16th century tower recently restored from ruin to make a residence. Here in the late 16th century lived the celebrated "Flower of Yarrow" the beautiful Mary Scott of Dryhope, after her marriage to Walter Scott, elder son of Scott of Harden. Follow the track past the tower and the steading of Old Kirkhope, and cross over the road onto another track. After 300yards turn right off this track and head up to where a double gate is visible at NT 368245. There's no real path but its not too difficult. The path shown on the map goes through a gate at 359246 to another at 352247, but in practice its easier to stay north of the fence until the junction of fences at 354248 and then follow a faint path SW to the gate at 352247. From here you can see the cairn at 346248. Drop down NW from the cairn and climb a gate at 345251 to get access to a track leading down to the SW corner of the steading of Sundhope, which can be clearly seen all the way down from the cairn. Take the track leading west from Sundhope on the south bank of Yarrow Water. The track ends in sheep pens after half a mile but there's a path not marked on the map which continues through fields (all the gates open.) Eventually there's a stile in a corner leading down onto B709 just as it makes a bend to cross the river and head north to cross A708. At the junction is the GORDON ARMS HOTEL, which has a bunkhouse and other rooms, and will allow occasional backpackers to camp.

Follow the A708 westwards for a mile to Craig Douglas than then take the track heading north to BLACKHOUSE. There are ruins here of a late 16th century tower of the Stewarts of Traquair. The circular corner stair turret is an unusual feature in this part of Scotland. Cross over the Southern Upland Way and take the track past the south side of the steading. After half a mile take the track up into the forest on the right. After half a mile a path is signed off on the left. It climbs steeply through the forest for two thirds of a mile. At the top there's half a mile of bog crossed by a minimal path following the fence to a gate at 264303. Follow the path NE for 100 yards to an indistinct crossroads of paths and turn NW. The path isn't well defined at first but gradually becomes an easy to follow track leading up to a gate at 271327. Ignore the well defined path following the top of the ridge, which is not the path that's signed. Either take the signed path to Peebles which is hardly traceable now amongst the heather, or follow the fence SW to a post marked by the author with the grid ref 270326, and take an even fainter path heading NW to drop steeply through heather. The path only becomes distinct after crossing a burn at 266331, and then heads north to deserted Glensax, from which a good track leads down the valley, only becoming a road beyond Upper Newby. You'll pass HAYSTOUN, a 16th century house of the Elphinstones remodelled by the Hays in the 17th century. Keep right at the unfenced junction past the house. Turn left at a T-junction. Follow the road round, cut across Victoria Park and B7062 to reach a footbridge over the Tweed. Go up Tweed Green and Tweed Brae to reach the centre of Peebles.

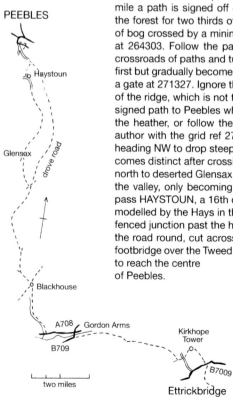

▬ Busy Road
═ Quiet Lane
- - Path or Track
⊙ Church
○ Other Waypoint

PEEBLES

Haystoun

drove road

Glensax

Blackhouse

A708 Gordon Arms

B709

two miles

Kirkhope
Tower

B7009

Ettrickbridge

Crosskirk at Peebles

PEEBLES - WEST LINTON   14m mostly on well signed drove road path, 3m of roads

PEEBLES (pop 8000) offers all services and once had a royal castle north of where the main bridge is, where a church now lies on a promontory between the Eddleston Water and the Tweed. There's a tourist office in the High St and toilets with sinks in an alleyway west of the tourist office. From the supermarket you can go up Bridgegate, into Old Church St and over Cross Rd to the ruins of Crosskirk. There are footings of cloistral ranges added to the north of the church after it became a Trinitarian Friary in 1474. Go west down Cross Rd and St Andrew's Rd to find the late 15th century tower of a new parish church built to serve the townfolk after Crosskirk became a friary. Go south out of St Andrew's cemetery, and cross A72 into Hay Lodge Park. Follow the paths along the north side of the River Tweed until you arrive below picturesque NEIDPATH CASTLE, a large 14th century L-plan tower built by the Hays on a rock outcrop. The outbuildings to the east are mostly the work of John Hay, 2nd Earl of Tweeddale in the 1660s, when the tower was remodelled. It now belongs to the Earl of Wemyss. Go round the outside of the tower and climb up to the drive down to it from the A72. Walk down the main road 100yards to find a footpath signed off on the left. Go through the gate on the right beside Jedderfield (this was the original name of the castle) and keep to the field edge as a sign tells you to do. A stile then leads to a path up through woods. On the open ground above keep round to the right, hugging the contour, to join a drove road path coming out of Peebles on the east flank of Hamilton Hill.

Neidpath Castle

Kirkhope Tower

Recently improved in several places, and equipped with tall new signposts, this drove road path comes out of Peebles town centre along Rosetta Road, the start of which you passed between the two ruined churches. It passes the Rosetta Caravan Park which takes tents. Between NT 232433 and where it meets a road at 226436 a new section of path has been created. Follow the road north for a mile, keeping right at a junction, and take the track up to a cross-roads of paths at Stewarton, where you turn right, and then left after a quarter of a mile (at NT 221459). After a farm the path climbs into a forest. Once over the top turn right for 50 yards, then sharp left on a forest track passing south of Greenside. After half a mile take the path signed off right leading down to a bridge over Flemington Burn. The path joins a track coming down from Fingland, and heads round the south flank of Green Knowe to cross Fingland Burn at 185467. It climbs up, goes through a small section of woodland, and descends as a track. When the track goes east towards a farm go straight on along a path down to Romanno House. A short road then leads to A701, but you can avoid walking on it by taking the new path beside Romanno House which leads through to a road through a new housing estate. At the end turn right, then left, and left again to come down to A701 opposite B7059, which you walk along for two miles to get to WEST LINTON. Fortunately there's a pavement for about half of the way. West Linton has toilets with sinks in an alleyway opposite the Co-Op, and there's also a chemists. Almost opposite the bus stop on A702 (buses to Edinburgh) is the Old Manor, a small and much altered 16th century tower house.

WEST LINTON - MILNGAVIE

58m. 3m on road, 5m moorland track, 5m roads, then easy 40m on canal towpaths. No campsites west of Linlithgow. No toilets beyond the Falkirk Wheel.

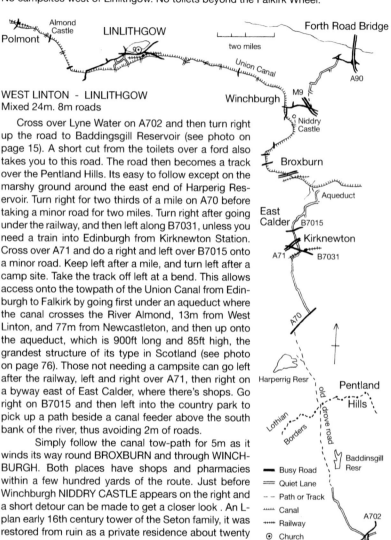

WEST LINTON - LINLITHGOW
Mixed 24m. 8m roads

Cross over Lyne Water on A702 and then turn right up the road to Baddingsgill Reservoir (see photo on page 15). A short cut from the toilets over a ford also takes you to this road. The road then becomes a track over the Pentland Hills. Its easy to follow except on the marshy ground around the east end of Harperig Reservoir. Turn right for two thirds of a mile on A70 before taking a minor road for two miles. Turn right after going under the railway, and then left along B7031, unless you need a train into Edinburgh from Kirknewton Station. Cross over A71 and do a right and left over B7015 onto a minor road. Keep left after a mile, and turn left after a camp site. Take the track off left at a bend. This allows access onto the towpath of the Union Canal from Edinburgh to Falkirk by going first under an aqueduct where the canal crosses the River Almond, 13m from West Linton, and 77m from Newcastleton, and then up onto the aqueduct, which is 900ft long and 85ft high, the grandest structure of its type in Scotland (see photo on page 76). Those not needing a campsite can go left after the railway, left and right over A71, then right on a byway east of East Calder, where there's shops. Go right on B7015 and then left into the country park to pick up a path beside a canal feeder above the south bank of the river, thus avoiding 2m of roads.

Simply follow the canal tow-path for 5m as it winds its way round BROXBURN and through WINCHBURGH. Both places have shops and pharmacies within a few hundred yards of the route. Just before Winchburgh NIDDRY CASTLE appears on the right and a short detour can be made to get a closer look . An L-plan early 16th century tower of the Seton family, it was restored from ruin as a private residence about twenty years ago, foundations of its court then being uncovered. For a backdrop it has a huge old slagheap, now mostly covered in vegetation. See page 68 for details of a route from here to the Forth Road Bridge.

Six miles from Winchburgh the canal reaches LINLITHGOW, where there's easy access to shops, toilets, and trains into Edinburgh. Historic Scotland administers the fine 15th, 16th, and 17th century ruined royal palace, with four ranges around an open court (entrance fee payable, which lies on the site of an older castle. In the palace were born King James V in 1512, and his daughter Queen Mary in 1542. Adjoining the palace is one of Scotland's largest and finest late medieval churches, a cruciform building with rib-vaulted aisles, a polygonal east apse, and a west tower bearing an aluminum spire of 1964, replacing a former crown-spire. Up in Beecraigs Wood two miles to the south of Linlithgow is a campsite and restaurant. Its a bit of a walk up to it but there is a very cheap council-subsidised dial-a-taxi service instead of buses.

LINLITHGOW - MILNGAVIE   34m, 29m of towpaths & 4m paths. Just 1m of road.

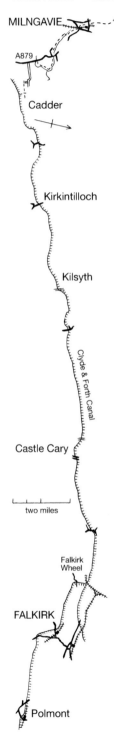

Three miles west of Linlithgow the canal crosses the River Avon, which forms the boundary between Lothian and Central regions. After another mile and a half there's a clear view of a ruined L-plan tower buit by the Crawfords in the 15th century. It passed to the Livingstones, who later changed its name from Haining to Almond. After two more miles there's a station and shop near the canal at POLMONT. Three more miles (note the interesting faces on either side of bridge 61 before the 630 yard tunnel) bring the canal to FALKIRK. A station lies near the canal but the town centre and the other station are two thirds of a mile away. The town has a population of 40,000. It has no ancient buildings now surviving and was latterly very much an industrial centre, but it was an important place in Scottish history. Here in 1298 Edward I of England defeated William Wallace. A second battle here in January 1746 on the slopes above bridge 62 was a Jacobite victory, although rather over-shadowed by their subsequent defeat at Culloden.

Originally there was a flight of 11 locks taking the Union canal from Edinburgh 110 ft down to meet the Forth and Clyde canal two miles west of Falkirk. Originally built in 1790, but closed since 1963, the Forth and Clyde Canal was restored as a waterway during the late 1990s. The amazing lifting device known as the FALKIRK WHEEL (see photo on page 5) was built as a Millenium project to replace most of the locks linking the canals, and it has now become a major tourist attraction, with a cafe, toilets, and an exhibition, access being free. You will arrive beside the Union Canal through Rough Castle tunnel and find yourself looking down on the wheel and a large circular canal basin. From the Falkirk Wheel follow the signs for the Roman fort, taking a path under the canal aqueduct between the tunnel and the wheel. Signed paths lead through to ROUGH CASTLE, where there are earthworks of a small square Roman fort with an east annex, both lying south of the ditch and rampart of the Antonine Wall, which survives for short sections on either side to the east and west. In the mid 2nd century this 37m long barrier briefly replaced Hadrian's Wall as the northen limit of the Roman Empire.

From the car-park serving visitors to the fort follow the track westwards to BONNYBRIDGE. Go under the canal on a path beside a stream. Turn left to regain the towpath, or right for 100yards to access a shops and a pharmacy on A803. The canal towpath is then followed to KILSYTH, scene of Montrose's last victory in 1645, where shops lie some distance away, and through KIRKINTILLOCH, where they are a bit closer. Between these there's a farm offering B&B at Tweechar, and there's the Stables pub beside Glasgow Bridge west of Kirkintilloch. Otherwise there's no services or toilets on this section. At NS 600715, a mile west of Cadder Church, turn right onto a path beside a tank. Turn left on a track and right onto the access road of a recycling plant. Turn left onto a minor (but busy) road for a mile to reach A879, go a short distance along it to the right, and then turn off right on the footpath following firstly the River Kelvin and then later on its tributary the Allander Water for 3 miles to MILNGAVIE. Follow the well-signed footpaths either to the station or the town centre, where the West Highland Way begins and there a fair range of shops.

MILNGAVIE TO FORT AUGUSTUS

124m via West Highland Way to Fort William and then Great Glen Way to Fort Augustus, latter is mostly track beside Caledonian canal. Both routes are easy to follow, being well marked paths signed with a thistle in a hexagon logo, so only a brief outline is really required here.

MILNGAVIE - CRIANLARICH 45m. Just 4m on roads.

Opened in 1980 as Scotland's first official long distance path, the West Highland Way has an obvious starting point in the middle of Milngavie. The way uses a green corridor leading north and you don't see much of the houses. After three miles you pass west of Craigallian Loch and east of Carbeth Loch. There's a short section westwards along B821, then the path heads north to join an old railway line, giving four miles of easy level walking. Two miles along a lane then bring you east of Drymen, where there's accommodation and a shop. A short path runs east beside A811 and then the route runs on tracks through Garadhban Forest. The official route goes over Conic Hill, although in 2005 this was closed for tree-felling and the way was diverted down onto B837 to Loch Lomond at Balmaha, where there's toilets and a hotel.

For the next few miles the route alteratively uses bits of road and loops of path out onto headlands beside the loch. There's two campsites on this section, the further one having a small shop. The going is easy apart from a climb at Ross Wood. At Rowardennan there's a hotel, and then a youth hostel, round the corner from which (25m from Milngavie) are official free pitches for single overnights by backpackers without any facilities provided. Beyond Ptarmigan Lodge you can choose between an easy forest track or a rougher path with better views further down. The path passes Rob Roy's Prison and Rowchoish bothy, 28m from Milngavie, last survivor of a group of houses. Rob Roy MacGregor held lands in this area and possibly used the prison (a natural cavity below a crag) for his kidnap victims. In 1716 he captured the factor of a former ally, the Duke of Montrose, who had had Rob Roy bankrupted in 1711 after Rob's head drover ran away with all his funds for purchasing cattle. Rob Roy evaded capture and died in his bed near Balquidder (where he is buried) in 1734, aged about 63.

There are more official wild camping places just north of Inversnaid Lodge, The access road to the lodge over from Loch Katrine to the east passes a former chapel now used as a bunkhouse (at NN 346092). Across Loch Lomond can be seen the pipes of the Loch Sloy hydro-electric scheme. North of Inversnaid the path becomes narrower, winding, with tree roots and steep climbs to slow down progress, whilst access to Rob Roy's cave involves quite a scramble. After 34m from Milngavie there's a wooded island called Eilean Vow in the loch with a ruined 16th century tower on it, and another mile brings you to Doune Byre, another bothy. There's a bit of a climb up from the north end of the loch over to Inverarnan, 38m from Milngavie where there's a campsite with a shop and waterfalls. Beyond here a good track leads up Glen Falloch, passes the Falls of Falloch and then goes under the railway and over A82 to climb over the shoulder of Kirk Craig, above Crianlarich.

Rowchoish

Rob Roy's Prison

Ptarmigan Lodge

Rowardennan

two miles

Conic Hill

Balmaha

Loch Lomond

B837

Drymen

— Busy Road
= Quiet Lane
- - Path or Track
+++ Railway
⊙ Church
o Other Waypoint

B821

MILNGAVIE

CRIANLARICH - KINGSHOUSE   24m, 1m on road

Bridge of Orchy

A82

Tyndrum

St Fillans

two miles

A82

Crianlarich

Inverarnan

Castle

Inversnaid

Loch Lomond

Rowchoish

From Kirk Craig a branch path descends to CRIANLARICH, where there's a hotel, youth hostel, and shop. Originally there were separate stations serving lines from Callander to Oban opened in 1873 by the Caledonian Railway, and Glasgow to Fort William opened by the North British Railway in 1897. Since they were rivals the linking spur line saw little use until after 1965, when a landslide in Glen Ogle to the east caused closure of the line from Callander and the lower of the two stations. From the West Highland Way above Crianlarich there are fine views eastwards towards Ben More, at 3900ft Britain's fifth highest mountain. The way crosses A82 after a couple of miles and makes a loop NE of the River Fillan. It passes slight remains of a 14th century priory church probably on the site of a church first established by St Fillan, who died on the Inchcailloch island in Loch Lomond in 734. The way then goes through the farmyard of Auchertyre, where there's wigwams to stay in, a campsite, and a small shop. Recrossing A82 the path passes through woods at Dalrigh, the scene of one of Robert Bruce's military defeats in 1306. There's a hotel, toilets, shop and campsite at TYNDRUM, 50m from Milngavie, where there's stations on each of the lines out to Oban and Fort William. Just before reaching the village the path crosses a bare patch which is the site of a lead mine worked from 1741 to 1862.

Beyond Tyndrum the route uses a military road built in the 1750s for 6m to BRIDGE OF ORCHY, where the station buildings now form a bunkhouse and there's a hotel further west. Crossing the old bridge over the River Orchy the path then climbs in woods over Mam Carragh above Loch Tulla and descends to Inveroran Hotel, a former haunt of cattle drovers. There is an unofficial campsite (no facilities) here. Still following the military road most of way, and climbing through the remnants of a Caladonian pine forest, the way then proceeds for nine bleak miles over the Black Mount and the west edge of Rannoch Moor. It goes past Ba Bridge to the Kinghouse Hotel, the last mile, crossing over A82, being on a tarmac road. Former proprietors, two hundred years ago, were noted for making huge profits out of illegal dealings in salt.

West Highland Way crossing Rannoch Moor

KINGSHOUSE - FORT WILLIAM   24m Two steep climbs. 2m of roads.

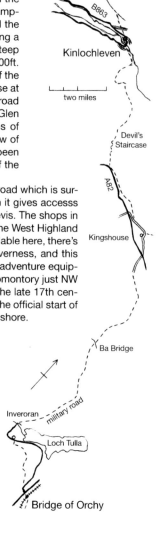

FORT WILLIAM

Dun Deardal

Lairigmore

Kinlochleven

two miles

Devil's
Staircase

A82

Kingshouse

Ba Bridge

Inveroran   military road

Loch Tulla

Bridge of Orchy

Crossing an old bridge beside the hotel, the way continues above the north side of A82 before climbing steeply from 1000ft to 1850ft on the Devil's Staircase, with fine views of Glen Coe. The lower part of the glen was the scene in 1692 of the massacre of about 40 Maclain Macdonalds by a detachment of Argyll's Regiment, mostly composed of Campbells, and the burning and plundering of the houses in the glen. William III had determined to make an example of Maclain after he missed a deadline of giving an oath of allegiance. Over the top there are views of the Blackwater reservoir, created in 1909 by means of a dam 1000 yards long and 86ft high to provide power for the former aluminium smelting works down at KINLOCHLEVEN. The way joins the service track up to the dam and descends beside the six huge pipes carrying the water down. Prior to 1900 there were few houses here, and the roads forming a loop around the loch were mostly only created in the 1920s. The town has several shops, hotels, two campsites, and a chippy. Until 1975 the River Leven formed the county boundary between Argyll and Inverness, resulting a curious duplication of services. From here there's a steep climb from sea-level up to the Lairigmore Pass at 1000ft. After turning north there's a cairn recalling where one of the Campbells fell after fleeing from their defeat by Montrose at Inverlochy in 1645. The way finally leaves the military road and takes paths through conifers to drop down into Glen Nevis. A short diversion allows access to the remains of the fort of Dun Deardail, from which there's a great view of Ben Nevis. The stones of the rampart of the fort have been vitrified or melted together as a result of the burning of the bonding timbers, probably during an attack.

The last rather dull mile into Fort Wiliam is along a road which is surprisingly wide and busy for a dead-end road, although it gives accesss to the car-parks, youth hostel and campsite in Glen Nevis. The shops in the centre of Fort William lie half a mile west of where the West Highland Way officially ends at Nevis Bridge. All services are available here, there's trains to Glasgow and Mallaig, buses to Oban and Inverness, and this is the last place you'll find much in the way of outdoor adventure equipment without making a diversion to Inverness. On a promontory just NW of the bus station and Morrisons store are remains of the late 17th century fort from which the town takes its name. Here lies the official start of the Great Glen Way, which then leads NW close to the shore.

Kinlochleven

FORT WILLIAM - FORT AUGUSTUS   31m via Great Glen Way. Just 2m on roads.

FORT AUGUSTUS

Caledonian Canal

A82

A82

Loch Oich

Laggan Hostel

A82

Great Glen Way

Loch Lochy

two miles

B8004

Gairlochy

Bunarkaig

B8004

Corpach

A830

Gairlochy

B8004

Inverlochy
Castle

Fort

Glen Nevis

FORT WILLIAM

Dun Deardal

Just east of where the way crosses the River Lochy beside the railway are the ruins of the Comyn castle of Inverlochy, a late 13th century quadrangular court with four circular corner towers, lying close to the battlefield site. The next bit of the way is a bit dull, as it makes its way along B830 and past a housing estate and school out to the start of the Caledonian canal with lochs at Corpach. You won't miss much if you take the lane past the campsite which then curves round NW to meet the canal where there's a flight of locks called Neptune's staircase. A wide track then follows the canal to the locks at Gairlochy, at the south end of Loch Lochy. The way then follows B8005 to Clunes, although a winding woodland path near the shore gets you off the road for most of two miles. Beyond lie seven miles of tracks mostly through conifers, although felling on the downhill side allows views of the loch from time to time. At Laggan Locks the way crosses to the east side of the canal, passing behind the youth hostel at Laggan on its way up to Loch Oich. At Laggan bridge (22m from Fort William) the way goes through a caravan site to join the route of the old railway from Spean Bridge to Fort Augustus beside the platforms of a former station. After a mile the way drops down to a lower track by the loch shore, since the railway trackbed beyond is rather overgrown. Hidden in trees on the other side of the loch lies Invergarry Castle, a tall 17th century L-plan tower house of the Macdonalds of Glengarry. It was burnt by General Monk in 1654 and blown up by Cumberland in 1746. Part of the ruin collapsed a few years ago.

At Aberchalder the way uses the old railway bridge to cross the Calder Burn, then turns back on itself to reach a lochside path to the swingbridge carrying A82 over the canal. The way crosses to the west side of the canal at Cullochy Lock, so that for the remaining four miles up to Fort Augustus it is mainly on an embankment between the canal and the River Oich at a lower level. FORT AUGUSTUS has slight remains of a former barracks, whilst the later fort became an abbey later on. There are several shops and hotels, plus toilets, a chippy and a tourist information office. The campsite lies half a mile SSW of the town, on the right-hand side of A82.

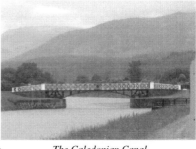

The Caledonian Canal

FORT AUGUSTUS TO JOHN O'GROATS

199m, alternating long sections of remote mountain tracks and minor roads mostly in valleys. Long sections without any services, accommodation, or even access to public transport are the 37m from Inchbae to Ardgay, and 36m from Lairg to Kinbrace.

FORT AUGUSTUS - ERCHLESS   30m. Two mountain tracks, 13m on quiet roads.

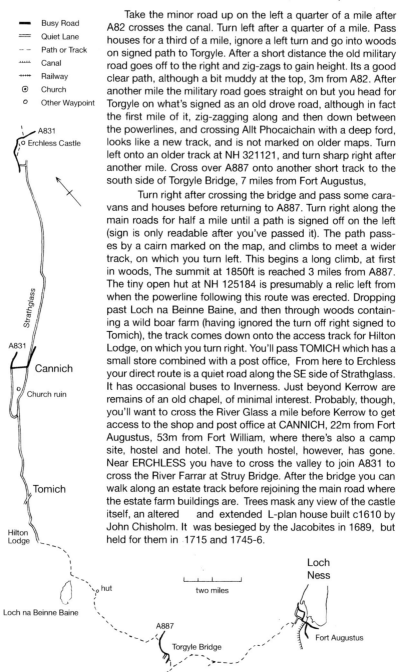

- ▬ Busy Road
- ═ Quiet Lane
- - - Path or Track
- ⌣⌣⌣ Canal
- +++ Railway
- ⊙ Church
- o Other Waypoint

A831
Erchless Castle

Strathglass

A831

Cannich

Church ruin

Tomich

Hilton
Lodge

hut

Loch na Beinne Baine

two miles

A887

Torgyle Bridge

Loch
Ness

Fort Augustus

Take the minor road up on the left a quarter of a mile after A82 crosses the canal. Turn left after a quarter of a mile. Pass houses for a third of a mile, ignore a left turn and go into woods on signed path to Torgyle. After a short distance the old military road goes off to the right and zig-zags to gain height. Its a good clear path, although a bit muddy at the top, 3m from A82. After another mile the military road goes straight on but you head for Torgyle on what's signed as an old drove road, although in fact the first mile of it, zig-zagging along and then down between the powerlines, and crossing Allt Phocaichain with a deep ford, looks like a new track, and is not marked on older maps. Turn left onto an older track at NH 321121, and turn sharp right after another mile. Cross over A887 onto another short track to the south side of Torgyle Bridge, 7 miles from Fort Augustus,

Turn right after crossing the bridge and pass some caravans and houses before returning to A887. Turn right along the main roads for half a mile until a path is signed off on the left (sign is only readable after you've passed it). The path passes by a cairn marked on the map, and climbs to meet a wider track, on which you turn left. This begins a long climb, at first in woods, The summit at 1850ft is reached 3 miles from A887. The tiny open hut at NH 125184 is presumably a relic left from when the powerline following this route was erected. Dropping past Loch na Beinne Baine, and then through woods containing a wild boar farm (having ignored the turn off right signed to Tomich), the track comes down onto the access track for Hilton Lodge, on which you turn right. You'll pass TOMICH which has a small store combined with a post office, From here to Erchless your direct route is a quiet road along the SE side of Strathglass. It has occasional buses to Inverness. Just beyond Kerrow are remains of an old chapel, of minimal interest. Probably, though, you'll want to cross the River Glass a mile before Kerrow to get access to the shop and post office at CANNICH, 22m from Fort Augustus, 53m from Fort William, where there's also a camp site, hostel and hotel. The youth hostel, however, has gone. Near ERCHLESS you have to cross the valley to join A831 to cross the River Farrar at Struy Bridge. After the bridge you can walk along an estate track before rejoining the main road where the estate farm buildings are. Trees mask any view of the castle itself, an altered   and extended L-plan house built c1610 by John Chisholm. It was besieged by the Jacobites in 1689, but held for them in 1715 and 1745-6.

ERCHLESS - INCHBAE 32m mostly on tracks

Follow A831 eastwards for a quarter of a mile whilst it bends round and crosses Erchless Burn, then take the track up to Erchless Forest Cottage, taking the left fork imediately afterwards. The track climbs through trees, and, 11m on, after much weaving, reaches the impressive Orrin dam. After the sharp bend at NH 436474 the track is drier and better maintained, running parallel to a series of water collection points for the reservoir. At NH 394486 there's a refuge hut left open by the hydroboard maintenance people. Continue past the dam and at NH 454524 cross the bridge over the River Orrin into the Fairburn House estate. Bend right after the bridge, then left at a crossing of tracks, and keep right past another building. Pass left of buildings, and go left at a fork of tracks and this will bring you onto a road leading past Milton Mains to a road on the south bank of the River Conon. Turn left for half a mile, then right to get access to a track over the dam at the east end of Loch Achonathie. The track continues around the east flank of Torr Achilty, and through the farm of that name. On reaching A835 turn left if you need accomodation or a meal at the inn, otherwise turn right for half a mile down to the shop in CONTIN, 50 miles from Fort Augustus, behind which is a camp site.

Beside the bus stop (hourly service to Inverness) opposite the shop in Contin is a path leading through to a cycle route along forest tracks following the north side of Black Water issuing out of Loch Garve. An anglers' hut offers a possible emergency refuge at NH 438594. Mostly dry and wide and well-signed, the track becomes muddy beside the north end of Loch Garve, beyond which is a connecting track to the hotel and station at Garve. Beyond here your route becomes a tarmac road to the humpbridge at Little Garve. Turn right down a road to meet A835, turn right and then left after a short distance onto a four mile length of forestry track. Turn sharp back right, and cross Black Water. Eventually you'll have to walk beside A835 for 400yards to reach INCHBAE LODGE hotel, but to start off with there's another 400yard section where a path runs west of the road. The hotel is 62m from Fort Augustus, 93m from Fort William, 367m from Appleby. An alternative route onto the four mile forestry track, adding over half a mile, but using a pleasant path through woods beside rapids, and giving access to toilets beyond a second hump bridge over Black Water at NH 402639, is to turn right on a path just before crossing the bridge at Little Garve. Both bridges are attributed to Major Caulfield, General Wade's successor in military road-building

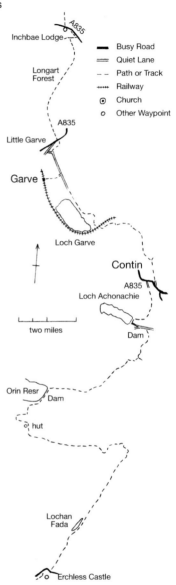

▬	Busy Road
═	Quiet Lane
─ ─	Path or Track
┼┼┼┼	Railway
◉	Church
o	Other Waypoint

two miles

The Orrin Dam

INCHBAE   -   CROICK   22m all by good, clear mountain tracks. A very fine walk.

250 yards beyond Inchbae Lodge turn right off A835 onto a track leading for three and a half miles up to Strathrannoch. The track continues out westwards to meet another track from A835 at Black Bridge up to run alongside Loch Vaich. This second track is actually a more direct route, saving a mile overall, but necessitates walking two more miles alongside the busy A835 carrying traffic for Ullapool and the ferries to Stornaway. A derelict house at Lubachlaggan beside Loch Vaich offers emergency shelter. To obtain details about two bothies within a few miles of this part of the route you need to join the M.B.A. See page 74. Ignore the track off right at NH366825, but after another half mile take the track leading off right past Deanich Lodge. Cross the bridge beyond and follow the track down Glean Mor for 6 bmiles. Turn left after crossing the Alladale River. The path over to Croick currently passes through the steading of Alladale

of Alladale lodge but by the time this book is printed the first part will be a new path beyond the burn east of the lodge. The path is good up to the stile at NH448903, then becomes a thin path, just about followable, through heather.

Cross the bridge and go through two gates to gain the road and turn right for 400yards down to CROICK CHURCH, 84m from Fort Augustus, 115m from Fort William. Completed in 1827 as one of 43 new churches in remote parts of the Scottish Highlands, it remains mostly in its original condition. Scratched on the glass of the east window are messages left by the tenants of the estate of Glencalvie, who huddled here in booths in the churchyard after being evicted from their homes in the 1840s, part of the notorious Highland Clearances, when the entire populations of many glens were cleared to make way for sheep farms. A gate leads through to the remains of a Pictish broch in a field to the SW. Part of the curving wall-face can still be seen. Brochs were defensible residences of drystone. One at Mousa in Shetland has walls up to twelve feet thick and 40ft high around a 25ft diameter central court,

Bonar Bridge

Invershin

ARDGAY

Carbisdale Castle

Strathcarron

two miles

Croick

Alladale

Deanich Lodge

Glen Beg

Strathrannoch

A835

Inchbae Lodge

Lubachlaggan

Loch Vaich

Church and broch site at Croick

CROICK - LAIRG   20m, all by roads except for 3m of riverside paths.

Follow the road down Strathcarron for two miles and then cross the river to use the road on the south side. You can use the road on the north side but the south side is quieter and after six miles there's an access down to a path along the river bank for just over a mile to where you re-cross the river at Cornhill. The access is down a private drive. Its signed walkers welcome. There are other similar signs later on after you've crossed a stile into a back garden and descended below footings of a broch on a cliff to the river bank, although halfway along there's a dodgy bit at the junction of two estates where there isn't a proper way over a burn and fence (although it isn't unduly difficult to cross them). Remain on the on the south side if you are making a detour for services in ARDGAY.

Turn right after crossing Cornhill Bridge and follow the road beside the Kyle of Sutherland for three miles, passing a WWII pillbox at NH593920. Beyond Culrain Station this road gives access to the youth hostel at CARBISDALE CASTLE, a splendid pile built in 1906-17 for a widowed countess of Sutherland after a dispute over her late husband's will. There's no road bridge here over the Kyle but in 2000 cyclists and pedestrians were at last enabled to cross without trespassing on the railway bridge of 1867 when a new walkway was added to the north side of the older structure. There's a second station and hotel at INVERSHIN on the other side of the Kyle, having crossed from Ross into Sutherland. Invershin is 12m from Croick, and 96m from Fort Augustus. The castle site two thirds of a mile NW is no more than an overgrown pile of rubble in trees by the river. After crossing the Kyle of Sutherland there's only a few yards of footpath, so you have to walk along A836 for nearly a mile, take A837 off to the left for another two thirds of a mile, and then B864 northwards for five miles to meet A839 for the last mile into Lairg. The B-road is quiet, most of its traffic being generated by the visitor centre alongside the Falls of Shin, which are rapids on the River Shin. Two miles north of the falls is a chambered cairn in a field beside the road. There's only short sections of river-side path, not a through route.

LAIRG lies 104m from Fort Augustus, 135m from Fort William, 228m from Milngavie, and 409m friom Appleby. It is a rather scattered place. The tourist office lies at NC 579061, and there's a shop at the petrol station south of it, before crossing the River Shin. Another food shop, a pharmacy, a hardware and electrical shop selling fuel, and the campsite lie on A839 further east, a third foodshop and the chip-shop lie by A836 to the north, and the station lies beside A836 a mile and a half to the south. This is the last proper shopping or drinking opportunity before John O'Groat's itself, as the petrol station at Spittal only has a few tins, crisps and sweets.

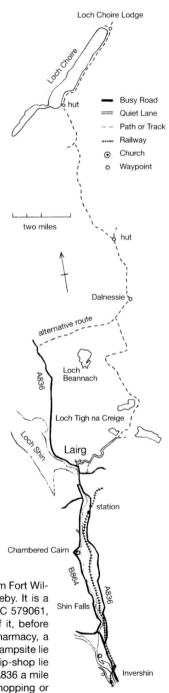

Loch Choire Lodge

hut

| Busy Road |
| Quiet Lane |
| Path or Track |
| Railway |
| Church |
| Waypoint |

two miles

hut

Dalnessie

alternative route

Loch Beannach

Loch Tigh na Creige

Lairg

station

Chambered Cairn

Shin Falls

Invershin

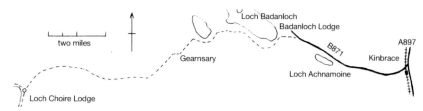

LAIRG - KINBRACE   36m, mostly wide tracks. One section of rough, steep path.

From the main junction in Lairg follow A839 east for a quarter of a mile, then turn left into Laundry Road. Go through to the tarmac road and turn right, climbing up the hill past Culmaily. Turn left on a short track to Culbuie, beyond which a path runs east of the fence, round the shoulder of a hill to join what has recently become a tarmac road for fishermen using Loch Dola, beyond which is a red gravel track blocked by a gate at NC 615081. Ignore a track off to the left, then at the next fork the gravel track goes right but you go left on a path to loch Tigh na Creige. The path becomes less well defined as it gets to the loch and isn't obvious after you cross the stile into the forest just south of the burn at the east end of the loch. Follow the burn until the second of two bends, then cross it and head up a path leading up between two disticltly different types (and ages) of conifers at NC 623096. This is easy to miss unless you look carefully. After 100yards through a conifer tunnel you come out onto a grassy track. Turn left, passing a ruined building at 622097 (not marked on map). Reach a sharp corner of a much better, gravel track after 400yards from the ruin and turn right. After another four miles of forestry track, some of it through clearings giving westward views, turn right over a bridge up to Dalnessie. An alternative route, shorter by nearly half a mile, for those who don't want to worry about possibly having to climb the gate at NC 615081 if it is locked, and the difficulties of following the route described for the mile beyond it, is to follow A836 for just over five miles leading north from Lairg, and then turn right just before a bridge for the track to Dalnessie running east in a wide clearing in the conifers.

At Dalnessie the track curves round the buildings and heads north. After half a mile it becomes a much less distinct path with other tracks made by farm vehicles slightly confusing things, although its clear where to go as you just keep close to the east of the burn. At the junction of burns and paths two miles from Dalnessie there's a refuge hut at NC 630187. Your path follows the western burn. There's a two mile fairly level section and then it climbs for another mile up to 1550ft giving distant views. Keep between the burn and drainage ditch, the latter being the best indicator of where you should cross the burn twice on the way up, since the path itself isn't that clear, although its not difficult until the steep descent starts on the other side. At 623241 the path was on a ledge in the gorge of a burn but parts of it have been washed away so for 400yards or so you'll have to find your own way beside the gorge. From about 623244 there's a clear path again. Ford Allt a' Chraisg Burn to join another path, and then use another ford to join the clear track with timber bridges running down the east side of Allt Coire na Fearna to where's there's another refuge hut at NC 619270 on the SE shore of Loch Choire. Then simply follow the track beside the loch, past the lodge, and then, after another ten miles, turn right onto the single track B871 at Badanloch Lodge. This road, with a walkable verge, reaches KINBRACE after four and half miles, Occasional trains from here allow access to services at Wick, Thurso, Brora, Helmsdale, Golspie, and the bunkhouse at Rogart, west of Golspie.

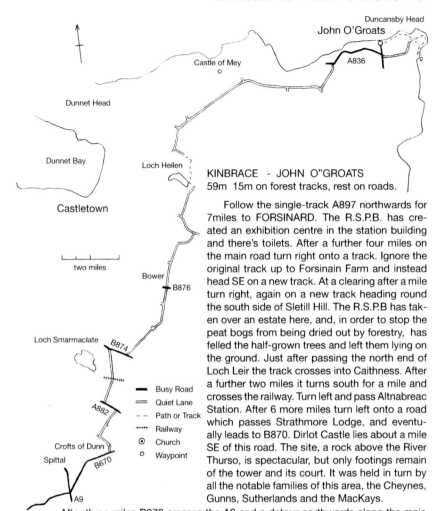

KINBRACE - JOHN O"GROATS
59m 15m on forest tracks, rest on roads.

Follow the single-track A897 northwards for 7 miles to FORSINARD. The R.S.P.B. has created an exhibition centre in the station building and there's toilets. After a further four miles on the main road turn right onto a track. Ignore the original track up to Forsinain Farm and instead head SE on a new track. At a clearing after a mile turn right, again on a new track heading round the south side of Sletill Hill. The R.S.P.B has taken over an estate here, and, in order to stop the peat bogs from being dried out by forestry, has felled the half-grown trees and left them lying on the ground. Just after passing the north end of Loch Leir the track crosses into Caithness. After a further two miles it turns south for a mile and crosses the railway. Turn left and pass Altnabreac Station. After 6 more miles turn left onto a road which passes Strathmore Lodge, and eventually leads to B870. Dirlot Castle lies about a mile SE of this road. The site, a rock above the River Thurso, is spectacular, but only footings remain of the tower and its court. It was held in turn by all the notable families of this area, the Cheynes, Gunns, Sutherlands and the MacKays.

After three miles B870 crosses the A9 and a detour northwards along the main road for half a mile brings you to a petrol station where water, other drinks and a few foodstuffs can be obtained (but nothing fresh such as bread or fruit). Two miles east of A9 turn left to Crofts of Dunn, and turn right in half a mile, After a mile turn left on A882 for half a mile and then turn right down a lane for two miles. Turn right onto B874, and left in half a mile onto a long lane which crosses B876 at Bower. Turn left at the T-junction at Reaster, then right in two thirds of a mile. After a mile turn left onto a track at a crossing of roads and tracks. The track turns a corner to the right on approaching Loch Hellen. Pass Lochend Farm, take a corner to the left, and turn right on a faint track over the fields to pick up the track pass Hollandmake, and turn right at Inkstack. Turn left after passing a memorial after six miles. Pass the youth hostel and turn right on A836 for the final two miles into JOHN O'GROATS. Turn left to get to the souvenir shops, the campsite, the Orkney ferry terminal pier and the hotel where the register of end-to-enders is kept. The food shop, however lies south of the road junction, opposite where another road leads off east to Duncansby Head. Via the route just described John O'Groats is 260m from Fort William, 353m from Milngavie, and 445m from the Border crossing at Kershope Bridge near Newcastleton. If you've used the eastern alternative route John O'Groats is 108m from Tain, 145m from Inverness via Munlochy, 254m from Perth, 290m from the Forth Bridge and 380 from the Border at Kershope Bridge.

ALTERNATIVE EASTERN ROUTE VIA PERTH & INVERNESS

220m from Niddry Castle to Kinbrace. Half of the 135m to Inverness is on roads and cycle track beside or close to A9. Scenic section starts at Dunkeld. Good selection of heritage sites to visit on this route. Mostly roads for 85m from Inverness to Kinbrace.

WINCHBURGH - KINROSS 22m Less than 2m on paths. 9m beside noisy roads.

To reach the Forth Road Bridge from Niddry Castle (see page 56) follow the path that runs around the east side of it, and cross over the golf course, passing east and north of the clubhouse to reach the access track to the latter. Follow B9080 east for half a mile and turn left on a track immediately after crossing the M9. After half a mile the track bends to the right and joins a bend of a road. You turn left, heading north. Turn right at a T-junction and the road zig-zags for a mile before reaching A904, which is followed to the junction with A90 at the south end of the bridge, where there's a motel. A tunnel under A90 allows toll-free access to the cycle path on the east side of the bridge.

After crossing the bridge drop down to go under A90 to reach B980 west of it. This climbs over Castlelanhill. At a roundabout cross over A985. Pass a church and then a Tesco supermarket on the left and then at a rounda-bout join the dual carriageway A823 for two miles into Dunfermline. There's pavements so its safer for walkers than the minor road further west up from Rosyth which is narrow and busy. There's a chip-shop on the corner just after the A823 goes under a railway bridge. DUNFERM-LINE offers all services and lies 151m from Appleby and 92m from Newcastleton. There's fine Norman work in the aisled nave of the Benedictine abbey church, famed as the burial place of Robert the Bruce. Little remains of the 14th century tower of the Scottish kings in the park west of the abbey but there are impressive ruins of the palace later kings added to the domestic buildings of the abbey, set above a ravine. The park also contains 17th century Pittencrief House.

From the roundabout at the NE corner of Dunfermline go up Hollyrood Place for a mile until it intersects with a cycleway on which you turn left. After just half a mile this leads back to a road to Bowershall, where you turn right into B915. After a mile this joins B914, where you turn right and then immediately left, still following cycle-route 1. It zig-zags up through conifers for two miles and then, having given a good view of Loch Leven, drops steeply with a hairpin bend to Cleish Mill Farm. Turn right and then left onto B9097, only to turn right after crossing Gairney Water for two more miles of lanes and then a mile of B996 into KINROSS, 22m from Niddry Castle, where there's several shops. The ruined castle on an is-land in Loch Leven can be visited by taking a ferry from the pier SE of the town. Famous for being where the incarcerated Queen Mary gave birth in 1567 to still-born twins fathered by the Earl of Bothwell, the castle has a 14th century tower and a courtyard wall which is partly 13th century and partly later, with one circular 16th cen-tury corner tower. Another island in the loch has remains of a priory of St Serf.

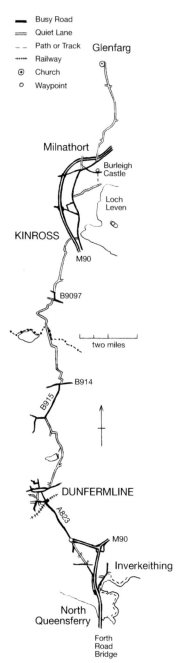

	Busy Road
	Quiet Lane
- -	Path or Track
++++	Railway
⊙	Church
o	Waypoint

Glenfarg

Milnathort

Burleigh Castle

Loch Leven

KINROSS

M90

B9097

two miles

B914

B915

DUNFERMLINE

A823

M90

Inverkeithing

North Queensferry

Forth Road Bridge

KINROSS - PERTH   18m. 3m of busy roads, 4m of hill-paths, rest on minor roads.

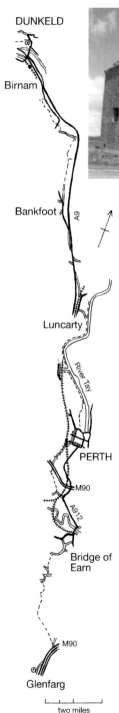

DUNKELD

Birnam

Bankfoot

Luncarty

PERTH

Bridge of Earn

Glenfarg

two miles

Burleigh Castle

Dunfermline Abbey

At the north end of Kinross follow the cycle-route onto a minor road heading east for nearly a mile, and then north. When the cycle-route goes east again carry on along the track going north. This leads a steading opposite the ruined castle of BURLEIGH (key from the steading) This Balfour seat has a circular corner tower with square caphouse dated 1582 joined by a length of wall containing the courtyard gateway to an earlier tower house. From the castle take A911 westwards to Milnathort, turn right onto B996, and then left onto a lane running through Duncrievie to Glenfarg. A mile north of Glenfarg turn left off B996 onto a lane at a crossroads beside the M90. After two thirds of a mile fork left on a track up through Lochelbank Farm. Pass a mast and a lochan, zig-zag down to turn right on a road to West Dron, Turn left and when the road forks left keep straight on along a path past woods and turn right at the bottom. After the road bends left take a right turn after a burn to reach A912 in the middle of BRIDGE OF EARN, where there's shops and pubs offering accommodation.

After crossing the River Earn A912 intersects with M90 after just over a mile, and then runs for two more miles into Perth. A more attractive route into Perth giving fine views obtained by taking the minor road on the left just before the motorway intersection. After the lane bends left turn right up a gated lane past a farmyard and up over the east flank of Kirkton Hill. Enter the woods over a tumbled fence (there's no proper way in, despite the path shown on the O.S. map) and follow the paths there to the bridge over the M90 beside another mast. You can then drop down through the suburb of Craigie and past the railway station into the centre of the town itself, which offers all services. With a population of over 40,000 PERTH is the largest town you'll pass right through the middle of, unless you made detours into the centres of either Bristol or Wolverhampton, although Inverness is not much smaller nowadays. Perth's fine collection of medieval monasteries were wrecked by a Protestant mob in 1559 and destroyed in 1652 to provide materials for building the Cromwellian fort on South Inch, itself now almost vanished. Now the only ancient building in the town centre is the large cruciform parish church of St John, 15th century, but much rebuilt. King James I used the vanished Dominican Friary as his favourite residence, and there in 1437 he was fatally stabbed by Sir Robert Graham.

PERTH - BLAIR ATHOLL   38m.   17m of pretty paths, 16m on lanes, 5m on busy roads.

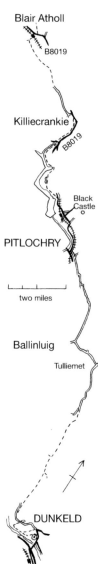

Leave Perth by the cycle-route passing between a golf course on the east and the much-rebuilt and extended BALHOUSIE CASTLE on the west, a seat of the Hay earls of Kinnoull, now a museum. After two miles you'll have to briefly join the A9 to cross the River Almond before there's access to a path beside the River Tay for two miles, passing the King's Stone, up to Luncarty, where you go through a housing estate (passing a shop) to reach B9099. Shortly before the B-road bends right take a minor road on the left to join the A9. There's no alternative to the busy main road or its verge for a mile until you can pick up a service road on the west side just south of East Mains. After a mile the service road joins B867 for a mile into Bankfoot.

Stay on B867 if you need the village shop, otherwise take the minor road forking right just after the ruined church and war memorial. Eventually becoming just a path, this leads through to Byres of Murthly. Turn left, and left again after a third of a mile, then after a few yards take a track on the right. Cross over B867 onto a forest track. Take a path on the right after nearly a mile when the path swings left and climbs the hill. The path leads through to a bridge under the railway and onto B867. After joining A9 either use the cycle-track as far as the station or the minor road to the east. Either way leads to the shops in BIRNAM. Stay south of A9 if you need the campsite at Inver. Cross the River Tay on A923 to reach DUNKELD, 56m from Winchburgh, where there's a better range of shops. Only the 14th century choir of the cathedral is now roofed, the aisled 15th century nave being a ruin. There is a tower at the NW corner. The delightful group of buldings east of the cathedral date from 1690, the original town having been burnt the previous year as a sequel to the Jacobite victory at Killicrankie. There's a tourist information office and toilets.

Take the path into parkland near the toilets and keep left to head west to join a road out to a hotel. After two thirds of a mile, where the road has finally rejoined the river-bank, take a path up the hill to the right. When you come through to a lodge turn left on a road for a third of a mile until there's a forest track on the right. This gives four miles of traffic-free walking with fine views to the west after the end of the trees in a mile and a quarter, although you'll still hear the roar of the A9 down below. Turn right onto a quiet lane to Tulliemet. Turn left there and after a mile, just before Ballinluig, turn right. After 2m turn and drop down to turn right onto a lane feeding onto another road (once the A9), Turn right to join A924 for the last mile into PITLOCHRY, 70m from Winchburgh, and 30m from Perth, the last proper town before reaching Inverness in another 79 miles.

Subsisting largely on tourism, Pitlochry offers all services, and has several outdoor clothing and equipment shops. You pass the tourist office on the right before anything else. The Co-op supermarket is hidden up a back-street on the right, in which is a chippy. The town is quite new, so there's no ancient buildings and the main attraction is the hydro-electric complex with a dam, and fish-ladder. Only modest overgrown ruins remain of a Caisteal Dubh, the Black Castle, a square court with round corner towers built by Sir John Campbell in 1326, which lies half a mile NE of the youth hostel.

A mile NW of Pitlochry you can access a nice set of paths through woods and past Loch Faskally. through to Killiecrankie. Here in 1689 the Jacobites won a victory, but lost their leader, Viscount Claverhouse (Bonny Dundee). There's a visitor centre with toilets and a cafe. Join B8019 northwards for a third of a mile, then take the lane which crosses the river and follows its SW bank. It becomes a track after going under A9, A footbridge allows you to re-cross the river and reach the centre of the village of Blair Atholl.

BLAIR ATHOLL - BOAT OF GARTEN 42m all on good paths, except last 3m by road.

BLAIR ATHOLL has several shops, hotels and a camp-site. Blair Castle, a much altered 13th, 15th and 16th century building, has been held by the Comyns and Stewarts, but since 1629 it has been the seat of a branch of the Murrays, created Dukes of Atholl in 1703. The ancient ruined church nearby is the burial place of Viscount Claverhouse, killed at Killiecrankie in 1689. Either take the track up the west side of the river from Bridge of Tilt, or use the path further east past Kincraigie. Go all the way up Glen Tilt for 13 miles to Falls of Tarf, crossing to the north bank beyond Marble Lodge. A path then leads over the watershed into Aberdeenshire and down past ruined By-nack Lodge. Ford the Geldie Burn (not easy!) and join a track to cross the Dee at White Bridge, 19m from Blair Atholl.

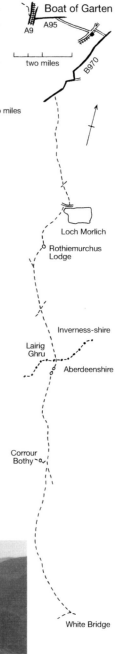

Turn left at White Bridge onto a path up spectacular Glen Dee, passing Corrour Bothy (25m from Blair Atholl) and going into Inverness-shire over the 2800ft high Lairig Ghru Pass in the midde of the Cairncorms. The mountains on either side, Ben Macdui, Cairn Toul and Braer-iach, are all well over 1200m (4000 ft) high, and often still snow-capped at the end of May. At NH951057 three miles beyond the pass summit take the path off on the right through old Caledonian forest to Rothiemurchus Lodge. Follow the track down for 2m to the west end of Loch Morlich. Turn right onto a road and turn left onto a track by a memorial unless you need the campsite, hostel and visitor centre at the east end of the loch. After four miles of forest, by which time the track has become a road, turn right onto B970 for two and a half miles. You'll pass a monument to John Roy Stuart, d1752, a noted Jacobite. Finally, turn left to cross the River Spey into BOAT OF GARTEN. There's a shop, hotel and campsite here, and the north-ern terminus of the Strathspey Steam railway running from the main line at Aviemore 5m to the south-west.

Looking back towards the Lairig Ghru Pass

BOAT OF GARTEN - INVERNESS 29m. Wade Road path, 10m on roads, some busy.

Take the road west out of Boat of Garten to join A95, which has a cycleway on its south side. After 2 miles there's a cross-roads where A95 goes south, B9153 goes north and you go west on a track under the railway and the A9 into the Kinveachy Estate. Turn right, then fork left after a quarter of a mile to follow the old military road. After twol and a half miles cross over a road (locked gate (but fence is low) to reach the hump-backed Sluggan Bridge over the River Dulnain, typical of those on General Wade's military roads of the 1720s and 30s. The route is now a signed cycleway and three miles further on joins a road alongside A9 near Slochd Summit. Either cross over A9 to stay on the Wade Road, now just a path (a modern track further west has replaced a boggy and heather-grown section further on), or remain on the tarmac cycleway down the west side of the A9 for three miles over Findhorn Bridge into Tomatin, where there's a shop, hotel and restaurant. Later on the cycletrack crosses to the north of A9 to use the B9154, but just before Moy you can take a road on the left, going under the railway and over A9 to pick up the Wade road again. A third of a mile west of Lynemore there's a deep ford across Allt na Loinne Mor. After another 4 miles turn right onto B851 for just a few yards, before turning left to another hump-bridge at Faillie, after which you turn left and climb up through conifers, crossing over a minor road. The track eventually becomes a road. Go straight on at a round-about when B8092 goes off to the right. You'll eventually come through to where the large youth hostel is at the south end of the central part of INVERNESS, 290m from Appleby and 231m fromm Newcastleton.

A royal capital as early as the 6th century Inverness lies on the SE bank of the River Ness and offers all services, with sev-eral hostels and a camp site at Bught Park 1m to the SW. From the station there's trains to Kyle of Lochalsh, Aberdeen, Wick & Thurso and to the south via Perth, and the bus station lies just to the north of it. The old castle was blown up by the Jacobites in 1746 and all that remains of it is a well beside the present castle of 1835. The only ancient structures in the town are the 16th century tower at the west end of the Old High Church of 1769-72, and the L-plan Abertarff House of 1593 in Church St, restored in 1966. A gateway off Friars Street leads into a small graveyard containing a defaced effigy thought to be Alexander Stewart, Earl of Mar, who rebuilt Inverness castle after defeating the Lord of the Isles at Harlaw in 1411.

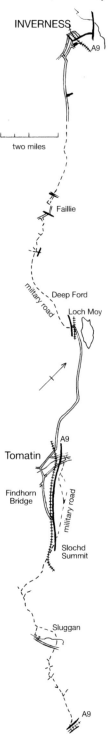

Old hump-bridge at Sluggan

INVERNESS - TAIN   37m, all lanes except 5m of main roads

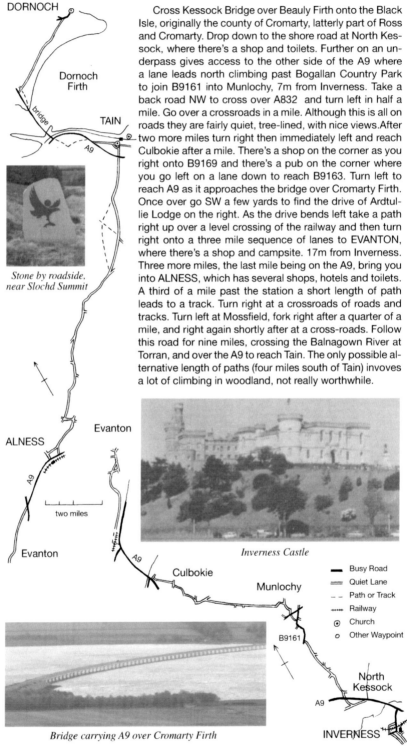

Cross Kessock Bridge over Beauly Firth onto the Black Isle, originally the county of Cromarty, latterly part of Ross and Cromarty. Drop down to the shore road at North Kessock, where there's a shop and toilets. Further on an underpass gives access to the other side of the A9 where a lane leads north climbing past Bogallan Country Park to join B9161 into Munlochy, 7m from Inverness. Take a back road NW to cross over A832 and turn left in half a mile. Go over a crossroads in a mile. Although this is all on roads they are fairly quiet, tree-lined, with nice views. After two more miles turn right then immediately left and reach Culbokie after a mile. There's a shop on the corner as you right onto B9169 and there's a pub on the corner where you go left on a lane down to reach B9163. Turn left to reach A9 as it approaches the bridge over Cromarty Firth. Once over go SW a few yards to find the drive of Ardtullie Lodge on the right. As the drive bends left take a path right up over a level crossing of the railway and then turn right onto a three mile sequence of lanes to EVANTON, where there's a shop and campsite. 17m from Inverness. Three more miles, the last mile being on the A9, bring you into ALNESS, which has several shops, hotels and toilets. A third of a mile past the station a short length of path leads to a track. Turn right at a crossroads of roads and tracks. Turn left at Mossfield, fork right after a quarter of a mile, and right again shortly after at a cross-roads. Follow this road for nine miles, crossing the Balnagown River at Torran, and over the A9 to reach Tain. The only possible alternative length of paths (four miles south of Tain) invoves a lot of climbing in woodland, not really worthwhile.

DORNOCH

Dornoch Firth

TAIN

A9

Stone by roadside, near Slochd Summit

Evanton

ALNESS

A9

two miles

Evanton

A9

Culbokie

Munlochy

Inverness Castle

B9161

North Kessock

A9

INVERNESS

Busy Road
Quiet Lane
Path or Track
Railway
Church
Other Waypoint

Bridge carrying A9 over Cromarty Firth

TAIN - JOHN O'GROATS 108m. 49m to Kinbrace all on roads except for 4m section from Dornoch past Embo. 9m in total along very busy A9. For 59m from Kinbrace to John O'Groats see page 67.

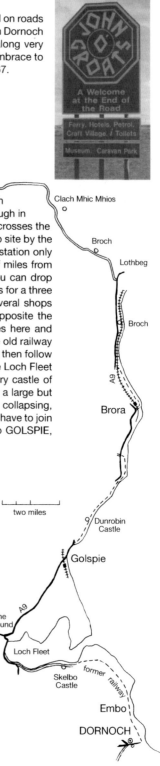

TAIN is a small town with a range of shops, hotels, services. There's a former collegiate church, founded in 1487 by the Bishop of Ross. Another chapel, perhaps older, lies in ruins in the same graveyard. Certainly older is the church ruin of St Duthus further to the east. The tolbooth with its conical roofed corner bartizans is of 1706-8, although in an older style. At the approach to where the A9 now crosses the Dornoch Firth on a new bridge of 1991 there's a camp site by the Meikle Ferry Inn, once the main building of a railway station only open from 1864 until 1869. Most of the two and half miles from Tain is on minor roads. After crossing the bridge you can drop down onto a track, and then turn right at a crossroads for a three miles of lane into DORNOCH, a quiet town with several shops and a 16th century bishop's palace (now a hotel) opposite the cruciform 13th century cathedral. There's camp sites here and at Embo, 2m to the north, accessible by following the old railway line. This eventually becomes overgrown but you can then follow a track to the tarmac road along the south side of the Loch Fleet Nature Reserve. Towering above it is the 14th century castle of SKELBO, a former seat of the Sutherland family with a large but low keep above a triangular court. One range, now collapsing, remained habitable until fairly recently. Eventually you have to join A9 for a miserable vergeless four and half miles into GOLSPIE, where there are several shops, hotels and a station.

Four of the six miles to Brora can be done on paths firstly through woods and then along the shore. You'll pass below the castle of DUNROBIN, main seat of the Duke of Sutherland. Much of the northern side dates from the 1830s but there's a central tower of c1520, and much of what you'll see from the shore is the work of the 14th Earl in the mid 17th century. BRORA is your last shopping place for the remaining 81 miles unless you use the railway to commute to and from shops and hotels. Beyond Brora there's a path over the golf links for two miles, but there's then a horrible three mile trek on the A9 (again without a pavement or verge), until at Lothbeg there's a minor unfenced road up Glen Loth over to Kildonan, 10m away, where there's a station. You'll see remains of a broch on the right whilst on A9, and there's another, more ruined, a mile north of Glen Loth, accessible if you can ford the burn. You also see the Clach Mhic Mhios standing stone. After crossing the railway at Kildonan follow the quiet single-track A897 past a souterrain (underground hiding-chamber) at Suisgill. After 7m miles you'll reach Kinbrace. See page 65 for the route from there to John O'Groats.

The Mound, at the head of Loch Fleet

Remains of a broch near Lothbeg

Kildonan Station

FURTHER READING

Follow The Spring North, Christine Roche, 2004
The Heartland, Queen's Scotland series, Nigel Tranter, 1971
The North East, Queen's Scotland series, Nigel Tranter, 1974
The Land's End to John O'Groats Walk, Andrew McCloy, 2002
The West Highland Way, Official Guide, Robert Aitken, 1984
From the Pennines to the Highlands, Hamish Brown, 1992
    See list inside cover opposite for details of books about castles and churches by Mike Salter covering most of the buildings included on the route.
    For further details of buildings other than castles and churches see the various volumes of the Buildings of England and the Buildings of Scotland series.

USEFUL WEB-SITES AND OTHER INFORMATION

www.backpackersclub.co.uk - Club for those interested in backpacking in the UK.
www.campingandcaravanningclub.co.uk - Join to obtain details of extra camp sites.
www.geocaching.com   - Finding caches using a Global Positioning System
www.forestofdean-sculpture.org.uk - Details of Forest of Dean Sculpture Trail.
www.hartlandpeninsular.com - Details of visitor attractions in this part of Devon.
www.hadrians-wall.org   - Information on Hadrian's Wall heritage sites.
www.ldwa.org.uk   - The Long Distance Walkers Association.
www.IndependentHostelGuide - Guide to independent hostels, new edition each year.
www.lynton-rail.co.uk   - Lynton & Barnstaple narrow guage steam railway.
www.mountainbothies.org.uk - Club to join to find out details of over 100 bothies.
www.nationaltrail.co.uk   - Details of long-distance trails in UK.
www.scottishcanals.co.uk   - Details about canals in Scotland.
www.shugborough.org.uk   - Details about Shugborough Hall (Staffs) and its estate.
www.southofscotlandcountrysidetrails.co.uk - Details of trails in Border area.
www.syha.org.uk   - Scottish Youth Hostels Association.
www.thefalkirkwheel.co.uk   - Information about Falkirk Wheel opening times, etc
www.traveline.org.uk   - Travel information throughout the UK
www.yha.org.uk   - The Youth Hostels Association of England and Wales.
National Rail Enquiries: 08457 48 49 50.   For buses ring Traveline: 0870 608 2 608
All Youth Hostels in Britain are open to non-members - at a small aadditional price.
Maps can be obtained through the Backpackers Club at a substantially reduced price.
The Backpackers Club provides members with info on farm and wild camping places.
Members of the Backpackers Club and the Long Distance Walkers Association obtain
    discounts on equipment from certain shops. Enquire for details.

Union Canal Aqueduct over the River Almond

The Gatehouse of St Briavels Castle